ESSAYS AND STUDIES
1974

ESSAYS AND STUDIES
1974

BEING VOLUME TWENTY-SEVEN OF THE NEW SERIES
OF ESSAYS AND STUDIES COLLECTED FOR
THE ENGLISH ASSOCIATION

BY KENNETH MUIR

JOHN MURRAY

FIFTY ALBEMARLE STREET LONDON

Printed in Great Britain by
Cox & Wyman Ltd, London, Fakenham and Reading

0 7195 3107 1

Contents

I

Past, Present and Pinter

NIGEL ALEXANDER

THERE is no future for the characters created by Harold Pinter. In play after play the curtain comes down on a terrible state of stasis in which the only possible development for the individuals concerned is, at best, continued stagnation, at worst, putrefaction. This is not a matter of accident. The characters frequently refer to the future—some of them may even be presumed to have an 'existence' to look forward to once the play is over. Yet the future which they imagine is quite clearly beyond their grasp. Their visions are perpetually betrayed by their actions—and their actions, as the audience come to realize, are conditioned by their history. This steady elimination of the future by the slow revelation of old times is the most distinctive mark of Pinter's dramatic technique. Its most interesting aspect is the way in which he subtly corrupts his audience into abandoning all hope for the characters. The menacing atmosphere of the plays is a product of the way in which the spectator is left prey to the pity and terror naturally associated with an unexpected visit to the inhabitants of inferno.

This mastery of technique is even more important than Pinter's grasp of language and it has not, perhaps, been sufficiently recognized. In an extremely interesting article in *The New York Review of Books* Nigel Dennis savaged those who sought for thought or philosophical coherence in Pinter's work but then found himself still with the task of explaining why.

There is no doubt at all that his plays *work*—that the puzzles they represent in no way prevent them from being extremely theatrical.[1]

[1] Nigel Dennis, 'Pintermania', *The New York Review of Books*, xv, 1970, no. 11, pp. 21–2.

The solution favoured by Mr Dennis is that the plays work because they are, purely and simply, exercises for actors—an elaboration of standard drama school improvisations.

> All playwrights must think themselves into their characters in order to put life into them, but Mr Pinter is perhaps the first playwright to think himself exclusively into the actor. It is this that he is 'obsessed with'. A dialogue such as the following:
>
> ELLEN   It's very dark outside.
> RUMSEY   It's high up.
> ELLEN   Does it get darker the higher you get?
> RUMSEY   No.
>   (*Silence.*)
>
> is virtually meaningless in thought or intellect, but put two good actors on the stage and see how it will hum—what deep significance, what frightening overtones, what enigmatic images it will produce. It is perfectly legitimate theatre, of a childish sort, and it is God's gift to the acting profession. An actor is not concerned with what something is about; he is only interested in how he can act. In Mr Pinter he has found a playwright who is equally uninterested in what the work is about: the work is simply the acting thereof.[1]

Mr Dennis is, I believe, right to attack those who seek to transmute the plays into the substance of the current higher metaphysics. There is nothing there, and it does a grave injustice to the more concrete problems of perception presented to us in dramatic form by Pinter. It is this dramatic form which Mr Dennis has ignored. If actors were really capable of making lines 'meaningless in thought and intellect' hum with significance the theatre would be a much busier place than it is. The lines are theatrically effective because they are in a context which is theatrically effective. They 'work' because Mr Pinter is one of those rare beings praised by Aristotle—the poet who is more the poet of his plots than of his verses. A Pinter plot is created not by intricate intrigue but by the manipulation of past and present.

One of the ways in which this is achieved may be demonstrated

[1] Ibid.

from *The Caretaker*. There all the characters believe in some miracle of rare device which will effectively transform their dreary present existence. Mick, the first character seen on stage although he does not enter the action until the end of the first act, is engaged (or rather says he is about to become engaged) in converting his old house into a penthouse containing

> Curved chairs with cushioned seats, armchairs in oatmeal tweed, a beech frame settee with a woven sea-grass seat, white-topped heat-resistant coffee table, white tile surround.

Aston, his brother, appears to have a slightly more methodical approach to the same problem. He intends to clear the garden and build a shed so that he can do the carpentry necessary to get the house in order. Davies, the old man befriended by Aston, has an even more modest design. He hopes, if only the weather would break, to get down to Sidcup to collect the vital papers which prove his identity.

These are all predictions, made by the characters, of what they will do in the future. The reasons that will prevent them from ever being fulfilled emerge slowly from the past. It turns out that Davies left his papers with a man 'in the war . . . must be . . . about near on fifteen years ago'. The effort to reach Sidcup may, therefore, be continuous but it is unlikely to be successful—even supposing that the man or the papers still exist. Aston's shed will remain a pile of wood in the bedroom while he continually visits shops or men to find jigsaws or other items that are essential before he gets started— a state of compulsive and nervous inaction which has already involved him in treatment in a mental hospital. Mick's penthouse will never have the colours of its 'teal blue, copper and parchment linoleum squares' re-echoed in the walls because he depends upon people like Aston or Davies to act as interior decorators for him.

It is, of course, possible for the audience to think like the characters and imagine a future where the journey was completed, the shed built, and even the penthouse created—but in order to do so they would need to disbelieve everything that they see and hear about the characters in the course of the play. Their behaviour is both repetitive and compulsive and the audience is soon in a position to predict what these individuals will do next. Their view contradicts the projections of the characters' fancy. The audience thus 'know' the characters better than they know themselves and can, with greater accuracy, forecast their future. It is bleak because it is blank. The terrifying contrast between the expressed feelings of the characters and their actual behaviour is the subject revealed through the structure of Pinter's play.

The meaning of the play does not depend upon some display of thought or intellect voiced by the characters. It depends upon the conclusions which the audience draw from the process which they observe acted before them on the stage. The fact that a Pinter play does not contain 'great thoughts' which explain 'what it all means' does not deprive it of dramatic or philosophical significance. The demonstrable fact that Harold Pinter has a characteristic way of structuring his plays is important because it reveals some similarity in the kinds of conclusion towards which he directs his audience. In the control exercised over the feelings and thoughts of the audience is expressed the dramatist's 'view of life'.

It is important to try to be as clear as possible about the principles involved since they are vital to the art of the dramatist. Actors are required to appear upon the stage, or acting area, for any performance to take place. The routine with variations which they go through is the act or action of the play. This performance could be entirely static—as a pianist might give a concert performance by sitting without playing a note of music. It could be completely improvised—depending simply upon the reactions of the actors to each other—although even improvisation soon has a predictable element. These are extreme cases and, in general, more control is sought over the dramatic performance. Such control usually implies an author, and a script.

The script, or play, exercises control over the actors and the performance in two basic ways. It provides information about whom the actors represent—what sort of people they are, what they are doing in their present environment, what they have done in the past to get there. It also predicts what they are going to do next. This prediction, as we have seen, may be of two kinds. It may be a forecast provided by the characters themselves or a deduction and prognosis made by the audience. In either case the course of the drama may fulfil or frustrate such a prediction. That, in its turn, provides evidence upon which further speculation must be based. The kind and extent of the information may vary. The degree of prediction, and its accuracy, will fluctuate. There is, however, no play written or performed using words which does not contain some information and some degree of prediction.

This provision of information and prediction by, and for, actors is taken to represent the passage of time—which may, or may not, correspond to the time taken for the performance. This is perhaps the most basic convention of all dramatic art. Although there are exceptions, the period of time represented is usually longer than that taken for its performance. All the essential elements of a performance or play may now be presented in the form of a diagram:

$$\text{TIME}(\text{dramatized}) = \frac{\text{ACTORS} \times \text{ACTION}}{\text{INFORMATION} \times \text{PREDICTION}}$$

This is the basic dramatic equation, if we may be permitted to abuse the language of mathematics, which every dramatist must solve in his own way. The fashion in which it is solved determines the kind, the style and the nature of the play.

Pinter's method is to allow the information which is supplied by or about his characters to contradict the predictions which they make about themselves until the audience is forced to make a much more pessimistic evaluation of their situation. This technique is hardly new, since it is the basis of the highly successful *Oedipus Tyrannus* by Sophocles, but it is not a technique that could be used easily by a man who was uninterested in what the work was about.

The Birthday Party, Pinter's first major work presented in 1958, uses a fairly crude version of this technique. It contains elements which are open to the charge of being 'merely theatrical'. At the seaside boarding house run by Meg and Petey, the deck chair attendant, there is only one guest, Stanley Webber. One day two strangers turn up whose names are Goldberg and McCann. It becomes clear that they have not only been associated with Stanley in the past—they have some kind of hold over him. In the course of the birthday party given by Meg for Stanley they succeed in subjecting him to a form of brainwashing, break his mental stability, and then carry him off to 'Monty' to be 'cured'.

Any audience is bound to speculate about the connection between Stanley and the mystery men. The lady who wrote to Pinter asking where they came from was, after all, making a reasonable request for information which had been provoked by the dramatist himself. An author who cannot, or will not, satisfy such a demand must expect to arouse the irritation of unfulfilled expectation. If the past is about to overtake and destroy Stanley Webber then it ought to be dramatized. It is not sufficient to say that the play requires their presence and the exact details of the intrigue that brings them there are unimportant. Spectators are not entertained by the dramatist's need to keep them in the theatre but by the logic and coherence of the pattern that he stages within it. If part of that pattern is simply missed out then the author is liable to be accused of using a 'theatrical' rather than a 'dramatic' device— one that is justified not by any necessary or probable connection with the plot but only by the fact that it is a play performed in a theatre.

In actual fact, although formal details of the intrigue or the 'organization' to which they belong are never supplied, the past is effectively dramatized. The opening sequence opens a gap between the aspirations of the characters and their behaviour that is maintained in increasingly painful fashion until the end of the play.

MEG	Here's your cornflakes.
	Are they nice?
PETEY	Very nice.
MEG	I thought they'd be nice. (*She sits at the table.*)
	You got your paper?
PETEY	Yes.
MEG	Is it good?
PETEY	Not bad.
MEG	What does it say?
PETEY	Nothing much.

What is established is a domestic routine of almost killing boredom. Yet Meg's enquiries about the cornflakes, and her interest in the girl baby that the newspaper announces has been born to Lady Mary Splatt, indicate great expectations that have somehow withstood the withering of age and the staling of custom. One of the reasons that she sounds like a silly old woman is that her vocabulary is still that of a bride enjoying providing breakfast for her husband and looking forward to the baby that she hopes will be a boy. Her unquenchable folly, and Petey's resigned acceptance of her good intentions, have a quality of heroism which survives even the laughter of the audience.

The placing of these laughs for maximum effect '—some girl [*laugh*], I don't think you'd know her [*laugh*], no [*laugh*]—' indicate an inspired touch for comedy. What is unusual is the use of this comedy to provide information which allows an audience to predict the relationship between Meg and Stanley before he ever appears on the stage. The compound of maternal sexuality in which her frustrations find expression is clearly dangerously unstable and liable to cause an explosion. Stanley's frenzied outburst has been predicted although its form will be unexpected. His own relationship with his parents has been uneasy. As he says of his 'great success'—the concert at Lower Edmonton

My father nearly came down to hear me. Well, I dropped him a card anyway. But I don't think he could make it. No, I—I lost the address, that was it.

He certainly does not wish to recognize himself as the son and lover of Meg's desire. The furies which seize him do not need localization. They have always been part of his history.

The ritual of the birthday party encourages self-expression—and the trouble is that what usually gets expressed is the hatred and self-loathing that lurks in every individual. At the party all speak in glowing terms of the past—especially Goldberg. Neither he nor the others can make it match the present or open a way to the future. Comparing Goldberg to her first lover Lulu becomes the architect of her own seduction. He visits her bedroom where she opens his briefcase and performs the part that she finds in it:

LULU   I wouldn't do those things again, not even for a Sultan!
GOLDBERG One night doesn't make a harem.
LULU   You taught me things a girl shouldn't know until she's been married at least three times!

Her position is both ludicrous and pathetic since she finds herself outraged and shamed by her own wish. Although she has been engaged in the same action as Goldberg they have been playing different games by different rules. The compatible qualities of Goldberg and McCann, sentimental seduction and mindless violence, are the source of their power. They gain control by turning all play into perversion. They need no further identification since they are an inevitable part of the circle in which each individual plays blind man's buff with his own desires.

In this context it is significant that Petey, the only character without fantasies of the past or future, is absent from the party because he is playing chess. His presence would have checked the wilder forms of the Goldberg controlled games but he can now do nothing to avert their consequences. Faced with the barely concealed threat of accompanying Stanley to 'Monty', Petey's weary acceptance and resignation can now accomplish nothing except to protect Meg, however temporarily, from the knowledge of her loss. The mysterious agents from the past who have deprived them of Stanley have not extinguished the ashes of their love—but there is no Phoenix to rise from them.

The Caretaker (1960) needs no such defence against theatricality. It is a masterpiece in which the pressure of the past bears down with increasing and unrelenting force on all three characters throughout its three acts. It begins with a prediction since Mick is first seen alone on the stage gazing at the objects which form the set. This is the collection of clobber which swamps the bedroom at the beginning and threatens to stifle their characters by the end. From the beginning a distinction is drawn between their behaviour— which is to live surrounded by these objects—and their vision of the future.

The first act is built round the rescue of Davies from the 'Scotch git' at the cafe and the problem of the papers which he left, fifteen years ago, at Sidcup. This information is crucial because it allows the audience to form some judgement of Davies. Aston refers to the man keeping the papers and asks 'How long's he had them?' twice so that not even the most wool-gathering spectator should miss its significance. It is clear that Aston's original good intentions have landed him with a problem. Its nature is explored in the second half of the act as Davies resents Aston's criticism of his 'jabbering' during sleep and becomes obsessive about the disconnected gas stove beside his bed.

The story of Sidcup and its problem of identity is so effective that it conceals, for the moment, that Pinter has given his audience far more information about Aston than he has about Davies. In the course of apparently random conversation three important episodes are described. One is a visit to a pub where he couldn't drink his Guinness because it was served in a thick mug instead of a thin glass. The next is the projected stroll in search of the man who may have the jigsaw which might come in useful. The third is the episode in a cafe where the woman he was talking to suddenly placed her hand on his and said 'How would you like me to have a look at your body?' Once they have been assembled they clearly provide evidence about Aston's state of mind. For the moment they do not necessarily cause comment.

In this way the revelation that Aston has spent some time in a mental hospital is prepared for without being actually predicted. When it is finally made, in his long speech at the end of the second act, the audience will react to it as something that they have always known or foreseen. From that there follows the inevitable reversal of roles in the third act where Davies is able to feel superior to Aston—'I've never been inside a nuthouse!'—and use him as the butt for the expression of all his resentments against the world. If Davies and the papers at Sidcup were the problem of the first act, Aston and his unbuilt shed seem the greater, and more menacing, problem in the second. The third act reveals that the real trouble is Mick.

Where Aston has the memory of the 'nuthouse', Mick has a vision of his penthouse. He hopes to use Davies as caretaker and as the man who will communicate the essential purity of his vision to his hitherto uncomprehending brother. Buoyed up by this fantasy and its apparent prospect of regular and undemanding employment Davies turns and rends Aston for the indignities that he has inflicted while helping the old man. This proves to be his undoing for Aston orders him out and Mick, perhaps provoked by his verbal assault on Aston, turns out to have believed him to be an interior decorator who had promised to undertake the transformation of the house. In alarm Davies disclaims any such intention. Mick promptly sacks him. As the play ends he is trying to secure his position by asking whether they will reconsider—provided he can get to Sidcup the next day for his papers.

The situation is the kind of psychological game tied into a knot now made familiar through the work of R. D. Laing[1] or Dr Eric Berne.[2] The situation observed and recorded by Pinter is both more complicated and disturbing than anything to be found in these observers of the psychological landscape and silence.

The house which they have inherited, represented by the clobber which clutters the stage, is the environment to which Mick and Aston can only adapt by retreating into fantasy. Since they cannot transform it, they have been transformed by it. The nature of their transformation makes it impossible for Davies to adapt himself to the role of Caretaker which he has been offered by both brothers. His own recurrent obsessions complete his destruction. In this play no one is capable of taking care of himself, or anyone else, or the house. Instead the weight of the past 'takes care' of them. The discrepancy between the information possessed by the audience and the predictions of the dramatic combatants make this a masterpiece of characterization. The audience, like Aston's Buddha, is apt to be left in a state of shattered contemplation.

The Homecoming (1965) is a play about a man who sets out to revisit his past. Teddy, now a professor of philosophy at an American university, brings his wife Ruth to the family house which he had left six years before. He is anxious that she should meet his father, Max, his brothers Lenny and Joey, and his uncle Sam. She does—and the result is that she stays with them to work

---

[1] R. D. Laing, *Knots*, Penguin, 1971.
[2] E. Berne, *Games People Play*, Penguin.

as a prostitute from her own flat while Teddy returns to his university and their three children. It is surprising that she should abandon her children, and strange that they simply do not enter into her calculations. It might be asserted that this, like the mystery men in *The Birthday Party*, is simply another unmotivated theatrical sleight-of-hand. Yet the playwright has taken care to emphasize that it is Ruth's homecoming as well as Teddy's—and as the play proceeds elements which have always been implicit in his drama emerge with sinister clarity.

Max, the seventy-year-old father of the family, is the character most obviously obsessed with the past. He continually regales his family with episodes from his past life—edited, or invented. As a tearaway, with his friend Mac from Aberdeen, he made people stand up when he entered a room since they were 'two of the worst hated men in London'. He had a genuine 'gift' for horses and knew Epsom

like the back of my hand. I was one of the best known faces down at the paddock. What a marvellous open air life.

He should, he says, have been a trainer and was many times offered a post by a Duke—whose name he has forgotten. He was unable to accept because 'I had family obligations, my family needed me at home'. He recalls the presents he nearly bought for Jessie, his wife, and the hard life that he experienced as a butcher struggling to bring up his family. This vision of himself and Mac as the twin manly pillars of their youthful London society is not supported by Sam, the taxi driver, who finally, under intolerable stress, blurts out

MacGregor had Jessie in the back of my cab as I drove them along.

It is Sam, however, who drops to the floor in a faint. Max's self image is barely touched, far less shattered. He has lived all his life securely insulated from facts.

Ironically it is the attempt to take over Ruth which now forces him to face them. In the second act she mentions that she was 'different' when she first met her husband. Max denies the process of change

> MAX   Who cares? Listen, live in the present, what are you worrying about? I mean, don't forget the earth's about five million years old, at least. Who can afford to live in the past?

He is, however, doubtful at the end of the play whether Ruth understands the bargain that she has made. Indeed he is beginning to have doubts about the bargain

> MAX   I don't think she's got it clear.
>   *Pause.*
>   You understand what I mean? Listen, I've got a funny idea she'll do the dirty on us, you want to bet? She'll use us, she'll make use of us, I can tell you! I can smell it! You want to bet?
>   *Pause.*
>   She won't . . . be adaptable!
>   *He beings to groan, clutches his stick, falls to his knees by the side of her chair. His body sags. The groaning stops. His body straightens. He looks at her, still kneeling.*
>   I'm not an old man.
>   *Pause.*
>   Do you hear me?
>   *He raises his face to her.*
>   Kiss me.
>   *She continues to touch* JOEY's *head, lightly.* LENNY *stands watching.*

> ### Curtain

Max is precluded from taking his own advice to live in the present. He is an old man and the weight of years cannot and will not be denied. He has created circumstances which he can no longer control and must, at last, admit that he is controlled by them. For him, in one sense, time has stopped since there is no way out of that final emblematic tableau created by the dramatist. Max is, in both senses of the word, fixed.

His identification of Ruth as the controlling agent is important. It reminds the audience of a pattern which has been developed throughout the play and which the dramatist now wishes to bring firmly to their attention. In theory the controlling agent ought now to be Lenny, the professional pimp with his flats in Greek Street and other areas of Soho. As an expert on the game he should also be a master of the kind of games played by Goldberg in *The Birthday Party*. But the game played between Lenny and Ruth at the beginning of *The Homecoming* has a very different outcome.

After their arrival at the house Ruth has gone out for a walk while Teddy goes to bed. On her return she meets Lenny, wondering if it is the ticking of his clock which keeps him awake. In the course of their odd conversation he tells her two stories. The first concerns the prostitute who took liberties with him under the arch and to whom he gave 'another belt in the nose and a couple of turns of the boot and sort of left it at that'. The other is an account of the old lady who approached him while he was clearing snow for the borough at Christmas and asked him to help shift her iron mangle. Finding it difficult he told her to stuff the iron mangle up her arse and, giving her a short arm jab to the belly, leapt on a bus.

These are most instructive stories—whether they are thought to be 'true' or not. Since they are improbable and incongruous they are bound to have a comic effect. They are also a bid for control. In her reaction to them Ruth ought to reveal enough of her character and attitudes to allow Lenny to operate upon her. Her reaction is certainly revealing but it is much stronger than the audience, or Lenny, suspected. His desire for dominance is expressed in the way he shifts the ash tray and tries to take her glass of water away from her before she has finished. He ascribes this desire for 'order and clarity' to his father—which reinforces the suspicion that these actions are a significant expression of character. Ruth turns the water glass into a triumphant weapon of her own.

RUTH   Have a sip. Go on. Have a sip from my glass.
         He is still.

Sit on my lap. Take a long cool sip.
She pats her lap. Pause.
She stands, moves to him with the glass.
Put your head back and open your mouth.
LENNY   Take that glass away from me.
RUTH   Lie on the floor. Go on. I'll pour it down your throat.
LENNY   What are you doing, making me some kind of proposal?

Lenny's self control is disturbed and he shouts after her up the stairs
and wakens Max. Because of the way in which Ruth wins this game
the audience will experience no surprise later when Lenny gives it
as his professional opinion that she will not be a tease when put on
'the game'.

In the course of the play Ruth wins another two important
games. The first of these is the philosophical discussion in which
Lenny and Joey are attempting an attack on Teddy. Lenny
begins:

LENNY   Do you detect a certain logical incoherence in the
         central affirmations of Christian theism?

Teddy declines the gambit by pointing out that it is not his pro-
vince. Lenny then attempts to start on the philosophical problem
of 'what is a table' which Joey reduces to the level of 'common
sense' by suggesting that they chop it up for firewood. Ruth
interrupts:

RUTH   Look at me. I . . . move my leg. Thats all it is. But I
         wear . . . underwear . . . which moves with me . . . it
         . . . captures you attention. Perhaps you misinterpret.
         It's a leg . . . moving.

The argument is important, not because it provides the intellectual
fireworks of the philosophical debates contained in Stoppard's
Jumpers, but because it takes the whole matter beyond professional
philosophy. Ruth is not talking about philosophy—she is describing a process of conditioning. They respond to her leg, her underwear, her mouth. She is in control because she understands exactly
the kind of stimulus and response which governs the environment

in which they live. It is an area of operation beyond freedom and dignity and it contains things undreamt of in Teddy's philosophy.

She understands it because she was 'different' and 'a model for the body' before she went away. Her past experience has trained her to win the final game—the provision of her London flat and the conditions upon which she will operate there as a prostitute. She has come home. In order to do so, of course, she has abandoned a home and in terms of the conventional wisdom, as expressed in the play by Sam, she could never leave her children in such a fashion. The fact that she does not mention them at all as an element in her decision draws attention in the most powerful way to the complex of emotions and attitudes normally associated with that relationship. This is, I believe, perfectly deliberate on the part of the dramatist. His audience are used to the idea that children might be a controlling force in a woman's life. He is now asking them to look at other forms of control and conditioning—and suggesting that the conventional wisdom only deals with a fraction of the powerful forces that shape and condition our lives. Powerfully conditioned herself, Ruth is also the instrument of control for others. As the play ends, Teddy has gone, Lenny and Joey are controlled, and Max is brought literally to his knees. For the characters, as for the actors in the play, there can be no further movement.

Old Times (1971) also leaves its characters motionless on stage. The elements from which the part is created are simple enough, some stolen underwear, a visit to the cinema, the way a girl has her bath, a girl's thighs and pants glimpsed in a pub and at a party, a man who one night sat sobbing in a chair in the girls' room—but the past turns out to be a more complicated pattern than any expected when Anna came to visit her old friend Kate and her husband Deeley.

Deeley was not aware that he and Anna had overlapped in Kate's experience. Naturally they begin to exchange memories of those old times—but the events are remembered with significant differences. Deeley remembers the 'bloody awful summer afternoon' that he popped into a fleapit past two usherettes—one stroking her breasts and the other saying 'dirty bitch'—to see *Odd*

Man Out. There was one other person in the cinema and as they came out he said to her, 'Wasn't Robert Newton fantastic' and they had coffee together and it was Kate. A little later in the act Anna recalls:

> One Sunday she said to me, looking up from the paper, come quick, quick, come with me quickly, and we seized our handbags and went, on a bus, to some totally obscure, some totally unfamiliar district and, almost alone, saw a wonderful film called *Odd Man Out.*

Both Anna and Deeley give versions of the night that he sat and looked up her skirt in the Wayfarers Tavern and at the party afterwards. Anna tells the story of the night that she found the man weeping in their room. By the end of the play Deeley sits weeping in his chair and repeats the movements ascribed to the man. The dramatist, as he flicks his characters between past and present, has made good use of his experience in films and dissolve and flashback are as effective on his stage as they are on camera.

It is easy to see why, in the Italian production, Visconti is said to have had sexual intercourse by all the characters simulated on stage. The tension between the three, the sexuality and intense visual imagery of their language invite such an interpretation. To direct it in this fashion, however, is to ignore its structure in which each act seems eternally repeated until the action ends, before the curtain comes down, in what seems like a still from a film.

Their search for the past, for the springs of action, has revealed only a reciprocating rhythm in their lives. Anna and Deeley have apparently had very similar experiences with Kate—but both accounts cannot be true since they appear to contradict each other. The similarity, however, indicates that they have both been adapting to the same environment—and the environment, the controlling force, in both cases has been Kate. At one stage Kate recounts how she remembers seeing Anna lying dead in her bed with her face dirty. Once she has replaced Anna by Deeley, Kate attempts to blacken his face with dirt as well. 'He suggested a wedding instead, and a change of environment.' The quiet decrepitude of their marriage seems close to a state of death. The arrival of Anna has taken them back to the point where the man sat sobbing in the room. It is a relationship in which, for all of them, there are only old times.

An art which eliminates the future is not likely to allay the anxieties of its audience. The dramatist who saps his spectators' confidence, however, also characteristically declines to deprive his creations of their fallacious faith in their own continued existence. Cabinned, cribbed, and conditioned by the past, they are never totally crushed by it. Their belief, despite all the evidence, that they can still win at the odds shows a heroic folly which may be indistinguishable from fortitude. Their belief in their free will, and the audience's awareness of their completely conditioned state, creates a remarkable dramatic tension. They endure, for our continued enjoyment, in this world of past, present and Pinter.

II

The Royal Pretenders in Massinger and Ford

PHILIP EDWARDS

That Policy hath never yet prevailed (though it hath served for a short
Season) where the Counterfeit hath been sold for the Natural, and
the outward Shew and Formality for the Substance.

Sir Walter Ralegh's Seat of Government[1]

I

THE purpose of this essay is to suggest some possible reasons why
two of England's leading dramatists, about the year 1630, should
each have been moved to write a play dealing very sympathetically
with the appearance of a pretender to a throne, who is in the end
defeated. The dramatists are John Ford and Philip Massinger, and
the plays are *The Chronicle History of Perkin Warbeck: A Strange
Truth* and *Believe As You List*. A connection between the two plays
was noted by Peter Ure in an appendix to his Revels Plays edition
of *Perkin Warbeck* in 1968. Of some features of *Believe As You List*,
he said, 'the thematic resemblances to *Perkin* are striking'. He
thought that, since the plays were given by rival companies at rival
theatres, one might have been written to match the other, but he
could not decide on a precedence. The date of Massinger's play can
be fixed quite definitely: the original version, which was banned
and is not extant, was completed by 11 January 1631; the revised
version was licensed for acting on 6 May 1631.[2] The date of *Perkin
Warbeck* is not known; it was in print in 1634 and was probably
written a year or two before that.[3]

A sketch of the action of the two plays may be helpful at the
outset. In Ford's play, Perkin Warbeck, claiming to be Richard,

[1] Ralegh, *Works*, 1751, II, 318.

[2] Malone Society Reprint of *Believe As You List*, ed. C. J. Sisson, 1927, p.v.

[3] In *Notes and Queries* for June, 1970, Peter Ure suggested that Dalyell's
reference to his pedigree (I, ii, 29–33) was inspired by a Scottish genealogical
controversy of 1632–33.

Duke of York, son of Edward IV, supposedly murdered in the Tower by Richard III, appears at the Scottish court of James IV, and is accepted there. He wins to wife Lady Katherine Gordon, who has the royal blood of Scotland in her veins. Henry VII successfully persuades James to renounce his protection of War-beck. Warbeck's landing in Cornwall is a failure: he is captured and brought to face Henry VII. He and his low-born followers are led off to execution. At no point in the play, by word or hint to others, or in soliloquy, is Perkin Warbeck shown having any doubt of the truth of his claim to royalty; and at no point does Ford introduce an incident or speech decisively indicating his own opinion of the claim.

Massinger's play, in the rewritten version which alone is extant, shows Antiochus, king of Lower Asia, returning to his kingdom twenty-two years after his defeat and supposed death at the hands of the Romans (in the second century BC). In his fight for recog-nition he is constantly opposed by the indefatigable Roman envoy, Flaminius. The Carthaginian senate, honest enough to recognize him, is too nervous to countenance and support him. Prusias, King of Bithynia, shelters him until persuaded by Flaminius of the political danger of his protection. Antiochus is imprisoned, humili-ated, tempted, but will not confess he is an impostor. There is a moment of recovery when a proconsul recognizes him and denounces the cruel Flaminius, but his defeat is final.

The extremely close relationship of the two plays has been obscured by the rewriting which Massinger was forced to under-take. His original play was about the Portuguese pretender who at the end of the sixteenth century was claiming to be the Portuguese King Sebastian, presumed killed at the battle of Alcacer-el-Kebir in Morocco in 1578. (It was after this that Philip II of Spain annexed Portugal.) The myth that Sebastian had not died and would return to his kingdom became very strong in Portugal, and the story of one particular claimant, active at the turn of the century, aroused great interest in England as in the rest of Europe. On the accounts of this pretender's adventures, Massinger based his original play. But in November 1630, Charles completed the Treaty of Madrid with Spain, and in January, Sir Henry Herbert refused a licence for Massinger's play, 'because it did contain dangerous matter, as the deposing of Sebastian king of Portugal by Philip the [Second], and there being a peace sworn twixt the kings of England and Spain'.[1]

Massinger refused to abandon his project and rewrote the play. He pushed its setting back a safe eighteen hundred years and substituted Antiochus for Sebastian, Carthage for Venice, Bithynia for Florence, Flaminius for the Spanish ambassador. Although Massinger used historical material relating to the real Antiochus and to Hannibal, the 'classical' play as we have it is a fiction; *Believe As You List* is a play on recent European history gone over with a paint-brush to make it look like ancient history.[2]

In the rewritten story, the indispensable element of dubiety is lost. Antiochus is no longer a mysterious pretender; he is the true king returning. The earlier hero, the Portuguese pretender, was, like Warbeck, an enigma who puzzled and divided his contemporaries, a famous real pretender of modern history.

If, therefore, we compare the play that Massinger originally wrote with Ford's, we see that both men took the true story of a pretender to a European throne, a pretender whom events and history had discredited, and invested that pretender with dignity and credibility in his conflict with the established ruler. Although in considering Massinger's play we can talk only of what we have, and not what we might have had, it is essential to keep his original purpose in mind.

II

Ford's prologue to *Perkin Warbeck* shows how conscious he was that he was reviving the outmoded genre of the history play. 'Studyes have, of this Nature, been of late/So out of fashion, so vnfollow'd . . .' Anachronisms though they may be, both *Perkin Warbeck* and *Believe As You List* belong perfectly to the tradition of the 'royal histories' of the English stage. I give a summary account of how that tradition, as I see it, is related to the period of

[1] *The Dramatic Records of Sir Henry Herbert*, ed. J. Q. Adams, 1917, p. 19.

[2] The original play sometimes shows up under the paint work; see the Malone Society Reprint, pp. xvii–xx.

English history which gave rise to it and, like itself, was rapidly drawing to a close.

The modern, secular, national state of England came into being in the sixteenth century by means of a monarchy that was as absolutist and deified as it could make itself. The new protestant nation was ushered in by a government claiming to be of time-honoured lineage, very old, very religious. The Divine Right of Kings, said J. N. Figgis, was 'forged on the anvil of the Reformation'; it was 'historically the form in which the civil State asserted its inherent right . . . and the independence of politics from merely ecclesiastical control'.[1] The figure of Christ on the cross was removed from the rood-screen of country churches and replaced by the royal coat-of-arms.[2] The country united itself round monarchs who were carefully sanctified with the unchallengeable status of divine authority. Elizabeth was as near the God of protestant England as makes no difference. England moved forward under a very strict régime which enforced obedience by invoking the full cosmology of the Great Chain of Being.

In France, of course, protestantism equipped itself with a political philosophy totally opposed to the English one of submission and obedience to divine monarchy; because in France it was not the Huguenots but the Catholics who were running the state.

The 'medieval' sacredness of Tudor monarchy may be seen as a magic to sanctify that which was essentially secular and essentially modern. The Stuarts took over the glamorous idea of the monarchy and supposed it plain factual truth. As Lawrence Stone remarks, 'It was the Stuarts who had to pay the political bill for the exaltation of Elizabeth.'[3]

Monarchy, then, was ambiguous in sixteenth-century England. It moved forward while looking backward.

The drama which grew up under this monarchy accepted kingship as its most powerful symbol. And because of its derivation, it was an ambiguous symbol, a Janus image, looking both ways.

[1] *Cambridge Modern History*, III, 750, 752.
[2] L. Stone, *The Causes of the English Revolution 1529–1642*, 1972, p. 65.
[3] Ibid, p. 89.

In Marlowe's plays, the image at times served for the dream of a liberated ambitious humanism, as in Tamburlaine's vision of the 'sweet fruition of an earthly crown'; 'Is it not brave to be a king . . . and ride in triumph through Persepolis?'[1] The image also served for a kind of ancient holiness which men degrade, desecrate, pollute, as in the appalling picture in *Edward II* of the delicate king standing in the 'mire and puddle' of ordure in the dungeon, then horribly murdered on stage. In Shakespeare, too, a king may be either a sacrificial victim like Henry VI or Richard II or Duncan, or the more energetic, practical and (for a time) successful figure who appears in different moral guises from Richard III to Henry V and Claudius.

It appears that much of Elizabethan and early Jacobean drama wished to present a kind of dichotomy in man, a bifurcation, or, almost, a split between the soul and the body, and it found the many-faceted image of kingship of inexhaustible use in exploring the dichotomy. In Chapter 7 of *The Shakespearean Moment*, 'The Civil War, and the Split in the Age', Patrick Cruttwell spoke extremely well of this division. He argued that 'the imagination of the Elizabethans anticipated the reality of civil war which their grandchildren suffered.' By 1649, the recurring *personae* of the drama of the age had received their incarnation in Cromwell and King Charles. The two *personae* were 'the military hero, the self-made conquering usurper' and 'the legitimate anointed monarch, the King by the Grace of God'. The one figure stands for 'the age's craving for individualist self-expression', and the other for 'its deep reverence for order and tradition'.

I have given elsewhere[2] my view of Shakespeare's use of kingship to define the two kinds of man, one from the past, an ineffectual saint, and one looking to the future, the politic, practical man. This amphisbaenic view of the king derives, I suggest, from the paradox of kingship itself. A Janus with two faces becomes two opposed types of man. The division is indeed a reflection of 'the split in the age' as Cruttwell called it. A reflection of its knowledge of titanic change, of its nostalgia for something old, beautiful,

---

[1] I *Tamburlaine*, II, vii, 29; II, v, 51–4.
[2] *Person and Office in Shakespeare's Plays*, 1970, esp. pp. 13–19.

unified, which was inevitably fading, the old lion, and of its wariness of the protean man of the future, who gets things done, the fox.

III

In a recent essay which is by far the best study of *Perkin Warbeck*, Jonas Barish has argued that the play carries on 'the continuing dialectic between two modes of sovereignty' which we have been speaking of, between 'the manipulator' and 'the one who plays the king beautifully', 'who dwells in an imaginative element distinct from mundane reality, and who fires our imaginations in response'. No doubt, if Warbeck had been king, he would have lost his sceptre like Richard II or Edward II. We should like kings to be like Perkin, argues Barish, but the 'politics of pragmatism' make it impossible. To achieve polarity, Barish suggests, Ford provoked a conflict with history. By making Henry VII unattractive, and by omitting Warbeck's confession of his deception, Ford forces us 'to re-experience events in something like their original disturbing density and ambiguity'.[1]

Barish has done a great service in insisting on the basic challenge in Ford's play. It is almost impossible for an Englishman to keep it as an open question between Henry VII and Perkin Warbeck: Henry VII was so 'obviously' the true king and Warbeck an impostor. But the openness is there and it is fundamental. The critical argument about *Perkin Warbeck* has usually been about the mental state of the impostor, the man who had come to believe in the truth of the role he had adopted.[2] These discussions make assumptions about the hero's origins which the play refuses to make. If we stay inside the play, we recognize that the argument is about two styles of life, each calling itself kingly: only one can be

---

[1] J. Barish, '*Perkin Warbeck* as Anti-History', *Essays in Criticism*, XX, 1970, 167–68, 157, 152. Apparently Sir George Buc (died 1622) regarded Perkin's genuineness as an open question. See W. H. Phelps, *John Ford's, 'Perkin Warbeck' and the Pretender Plays 1634–1746*, unpublished Ph.D. dissertation, Princeton, 1965.

[2] The most interesting discussions in this kind are by Ure, in his Revels Plays edition, 1968, p. lxxix, and by Clifford Leech in *John Ford and the Drama of his Time*, 1957, p. 93.

the true one, and Ford insists that 'legitimacy' is a red herring in the competition to discern the counterfeit.

Anyone who reads Bacon's life of Henry VII, a main source for Ford, is struck not only by the king's unattractiveness, but by the uncertainty of his title. In the first part of his narrative, Bacon shows the victor of Bosworth, *de facto* king, debating how best to lay claim to legitimacy. There was his own right, as of the house of Lancaster, but that had been 'a title condemned by Parliament' and it opened up the equally legal claims of the scions of York. There were the rights of his future wife, Elizabeth, whom 'the party that brought him in' had arranged for him to marry; these gave him but a courtesy right to the throne. Finally, there were the sheer rights of conquest. This hesitation and self-debate are worth remembering in the opening scene of *Perkin Warbeck*, in which Henry is addressed with all the worship which we have learned to associate with the Tudor view of the sacredness of its own house. Durham gives us the second speech of the play:

> *Mercie* did gently sheath the sword of *Iustice*,
> In lending to this bloud-shrunck Common-wealth
> A new soule, new birth in your *Sacred person*.
> (I, i, 24–6)[1]

Since one voice in the chorus of obsequious attendants is that of Stanley, who is actually supporting Warbeck, we may wonder whether these adulations are not presented with some irony. If we look closely at the third speech in the play, it is fairly clear that Ford is proposing something more than a conventional view of the providential role of Henry VII. The speech is Daubeney's, and it is of critical importance.

> *Edward* the fourth after a doubtfull fortune
> Yeelded to nature; leaving to his sonnes

[1] Quotations from *Perkin Warbeck* are taken direct from the 1634 Quarto (facsimile in 'The English Experience' series) because of the importance of the original use of capitals and italics. Line numbering is from the Revels Plays edition.

> *Edward* and *Richard*, the inheritance
> Of a most bloudy purchase; these young Princes
> *Richard* the Tirant their vnnaturall Vncle
> Forc'd to a violent graue, so just is Heauen.
> Him hath your Majestie by your owne arme
> Divinely strengthen'd, pulld from his *Boares stie*
> And strucke the black Vsurper to a Carkasse.
>
> (I, i, 27–35)

Peter Ure could not believe that 'so just is Heauen' (in the sixth line) referred to the violent death of the princes in the Tower, and he altered the punctuation to make it belong to the succeeding sentence! But the sycophant Daubeney has less difficulty in seeing the hand of heaven in their death. Their father took the throne following the murder of Henry VI. Their death was a punishment for the crimes of their fathers. Richard III's violent death at the hands of Henry Richmond was *his* divine punishment. It is very difficult indeed to take seriously any theory of divine intervention after this barbarous speech. And the position of Henry as a violent usurper himself is made embarrassingly clear. That Henry was an adventurer is the burden of Warbeck's charge to his face in Act v, Scene ii.

> —*Bosworth field*:
> Where at an instant, to the worlds amazement,
> A morne to *Richmond*, and a night to *Richard*
> Appear'd at once: the tale is soone applyde:
> Fate which crown'd these attempts when lest assur'd,
> Might haue befriended *others*, like resolv'd.

Daubeney's speech contains a further startling implication. Even if Warbeck *is* the man he claims to be, Richard of York, his claim is no more rightful than Henry's, being claimed by blood spilt rather than blood in his veins. At best, Henry the usurper faces Richard the son of the usurper.

The unimportance of 'blood in the veins' is further underlined in the exchange between Huntley and Dalyell on pedigrees in Act I, Scene ii. Huntley had married a princess, so his daughter

Katherine has royal blood: for this reason, the non-royal Dalyell is not to be allowed to marry her. But Dalyell says he's a descendant of Adam Mure,

> whose daughter, was the mother
> *To him* who first begot the race of *Iameses*,
> That sway the Scepter to this very day.

The implication is that if we're to take our stand on descent, then royal blood is, like an Irish grandmother in America, owned by everyone. The oblique compliment to Charles I begins to look left-handed.

The first point to be established, then, is that by keeping the descent of Warbeck open during the play, and by questioning the divine and historical *right* of Henry VII to the throne, Ford manages to balance his great opposites, and leaves his audience to decide who is truly royal. Henry has a bad time of it, and we should be clear how markedly Ford places him in the machiavellian camp. His strength and ruthlessness are clear even in the compliments to him, as we see in Daubeney's speech—'strucke the black Vsurper to a Carkasse'. He is a statesman of great ability and foresight; he has a very good intelligence-network, and he knows the value of the appearance of clemency. The second scene of Act II is classic. Stanley's plot has been discovered: Henry piously hopes that the traitor may find mercy, but allows himself to be persuaded by the Bishop of Durham that mercy would be dangerous. As Stanley enters, Henry quickly exits, for 'If a' speake to me,/I could denie him nothing'.

Henry's masterpiece, of course, is detaching King James of Scotland from Warbeck. It is done by Pedro Hialas, envoy of Spain, who is well bribed by Henry. Hialas persuades James of the beauty of a Christian peace in Europe (IV, iii, 1–16). James regretfully acknowledges that 'a general peace' is a greater good than the one thing which stands in its way, his protection of Warbeck. All the high talk is undercut within the scene by the references to the real motives of self-interest in each of the three parties, Spain, Scotland and England. James delightedly rehearses what he's got, 'and all/For *Warbeck* not delivered, but dismist?/Wee could not wish it better'. He tells Warbeck that 'the dignitie of State directs our wisedome' (it is interesting to observe how the words 'wise' and 'wisdom' are used throughout the play with connotations of cunning and policy). Henry has lured James (IV, iv, 24–31) into casting off Warbeck, and it has all been done in the most high-minded way. That James has given preference to a lower human value, statecraft, over the higher one of trust and friendship is made absolutely clear (IV, iii, 35–49).

Against the powerful figure of the resourceful and successful politician, surrounded by flatterers telling him he can do no wrong, stands the saintly Warbeck, who spontaneously wins the admiration of those who can gain nothing from him. King James speaks of his reaction to Warbeck as 'instinct of soveraigntie' (II, iii, 42) and contrasts 'kingly York' with 'Welsh Harry' (II, iii, 60–64). There is no need to emphasize the dignity of Warbeck's bearing, his sincerity and attractiveness, since these are so obvious. Katherine's love for him is the seal on his integrity and worth, and her fidelity a denial of those who accuse him of deception.

> *Harrie Richmond*!
> A womans faith, hath robd thy fame of triumph.
> (v, iii, 101–2)

True love and royalty stand as mutually enforcing metaphors. The love is a symbol of majesty: majesty is a way of describing love. This exchange of realities and metaphors may clearly be seen in the two major scenes between Warbeck and Katherine, in Act III, Scene ii, and Act v, Scene iii. In strong contrast, Henry appears alone (Bacon had spoken of his coldness to his wife Elizabeth; *Works*, 1826, v, 19); and his thinly-veiled offer to make Katherine his mistress (v, ii, 152–157) further distinguishes his concept of personal relationships from Warbeck's.

For modern readers, there is a certain effeminacy in Ford's picture of the 'new king': his delicacy and frailty could not be further removed from the strength of an earlier picture of a new king, Tamburlaine. Perhaps Ford meant to qualify a too-extreme

contrast. Henry's ability to rule, his firmness and control, are not
the parts of a villain, and Warbeck's sensitivity occasionally meets
some justified Scottish rebukes. But in the main, the play's contrast
between the ruler and the claimant is, in personal terms, entirely
on the side of the claimant.

IV

In Massinger's play,[1] the contrast between policy and personal
worth is even more marked. 'Romes incrochinge empire' (114) is
one of materialism and self-interest on the widest scale. Flaminius
is an enthusiastic and dedicated servant of the *idea* of the Roman
empire:

> In the brasse leau'd booke of fate it was set downe
> The earth showlde know noe soveraigne but Rome.
>
> (467–8)

His role dictates its own scale of values:

> By my birth,
> I am bounde to serue thee, Rome, and what I doe
> Necessitie of state compells mee to.
>
> (729–31)

In the 'labirinth/Of politicque windinges' in which this necessity
of state involves him, he has to become 'a Protean actor' (1203–05).
He warns Marcellus that anyone in power must remember 'your
faculties are the states, and not your owne' (2574).

The maintenance of Rome's hegemony demands that the
returned Antiochus get no credence, or, if he gets credence, no
support. It proves all too easy for the agent of an all-powerful
state to persuade subject people where their interest lies, however
reluctant they may be to deny what they know to be true; and
where persuasion fails, intimidation works. Prusias, King of
Bithynia, receives Antiochus with open arms. When Flaminius

---

[1] Quotations from *Believe As You List* are taken from the Malone Society
Reprint, with minor adjustments of spelling, punctuation, and capitalizing of
the first letters of verse-lines. The numbering is continuous throughout the play.

asks him to renounce his guest, he indignantly repudiates him: 'Shall I for your endes/Infringe my princelye word? . . . I will not buy your amitie at such losse.' (1598–1604). But when Flaminius offers him the choice of giving up Antiochus, or war, Prusias yields. Then Antiochus enters:

PRUSIAS	I am sorrie.
ANTIOCHUS	Sorrie? For what? That you had an intent
	To bee a good, and iust prince? are compassion
	And charitie growne crimes?
PRUSIAS	The gods can witnesse
	How much I would doe for you. And but that
	Necessitie of state—
ANTIOCHUS	Make not the gods
	Guiltie of your breach of faith, from them you finde not
	Trecherie commanded . . .

(1698–1707)

The contest between Antiochus and Flaminius, as the former seeks the recognition and support which the latter must prevent, is extremely well presented, because the struggle is one-sided only in the outcome, and not in moral terms.[1] Either Rome or Antiochus is a lie or a fiction: there is no room for both, and one must displace the other (964–969). Antiochus has returned from the life of contemplation to serve his country, to rescue it from vassalage.

> The Genivs of my cuntrie, made a slaue,
> Like a weepinge mother seemes to kneele before mee,
> Wringeinge her manacled handes.
>
> (56–58)

His kingly bearing wins an immediate response: true majesty cannot be concealed (907, 2317). Everywhere he wins moral victory, but practical defeat. Flaminius hounds and pursues him. When finally he has him in his power, his business is to uncreate him, to get him to unsay himself and declare himself counterfeit.

---

[1] Roma Gill, in '"Necessitie of State": Massinger's *Believe As You List*', *English Studies*, XLVI, 1965, 407–16, argues that in Flaminius Massinger presents a serious and not unfavourable incarnation of Machiavelli's ideal ruler.

Temptations have no effect. and Flaminius turns to duress: he humiliates and degrades him before the people and then sends him to the galleys.

> Is it not sufficient
> That the lockes of this once royall head are shau'd off
> My glorious robes chang'd to this slavishe habit,
> This hande that graspd a scepter manaclde,
> Or that I haue bene as a spectacle
> Exposde to publicque scorne . . .?
> . . . . Doe what you please.
> I am in your power, but still Antiochus,
> Kinge of the lower Asia, noe impostor.
>
> (2335–40; 2354–56)

V

Massinger was much more of a political dramatist than Ford. During his whole career, he was dealing with political themes in his plays, many of them directly or indirectly topical, and he was several times in trouble with the authorities for coming too close to reality for comfort, as in *Believe As You List*. The early collaboration with Fletcher, *Sir John van Olden Barnavelt*, dealing with contemporary events in the Netherlands, was banned outright by the Bishop of London. Charles I himself refused to allow a license for *The King and the Subject* (not extant) in 1638 because a speech in it, referring to a forced loan, was 'too insolent'.[1] Some speeches in *The Bondman* became a kind of national inheritance, to be brought out in critical times like those when there was fear of a Napoleonic invasion.[2] Even a comedy like *The Great Duke of Florence* (1627) is throughout preoccupied with the problem of absolutism. A Byzantine tragicomedy, *The Emperor of the East* (1631) contains a strange satiric interlude on the way projectors and informers (so indispensable a feature of the English court) were corrupting the empire. It is scarcely possible to think that the highly developed concern for national honourableness so prominent in *The Bondman* and *The Maid of Honour*, and the accompany-

---

[1] *The Dramatic Records of Sir Henry Herbert*, pp. 22–3.
[2] See the Introduction to B. T. Spencer's edition of *The Bondman*, 1932.

ing contempt for the moral failings of the mighty, had nothing to do with Massinger's opinion of English society.

S. R. Gardiner rather innocently supposed that many of Massinger's plays could be read as allegories in which James, Charles, Buckingham and the Elector Frederick play prominent parts.[1] He argued that Massinger's connection with the Pembroke family would have led him to support, as Pembroke did, the anti-Spanish and anti-Buckingham party at court which wanted more positive assistance for the Elector Palatine. Gardiner's identifications are absurd on two grounds. First, if Massinger *had* in such thin disguise criticized James and Buckingham he would never have survived; secondly, the proposed allegories can involve total misreadings of the plays.[2] Yet Gardiner's essay is important: that the historian who knew more about this period than any previous or subsequent scholar should have had, as he read Massinger's plays, the constant feeling of echoes of real situations is something which cannot be overlooked. Gardiner made the mistake of pushing too hard: had he been content with topicality at a deeper level, his essay would have told us more about the political reference of Massinger's plays than it does.

What was there, then, in the spirit of the times which might have influenced Massinger, and by implication Ford, in fashioning his pretender play?

The years preceding the signing of the Treaty of Madrid in 1630 were years in which growing anger at Charles's autocratic attempts to raise money without the help of Parliament was coupled with humiliation and shame at the disgraceful failures of English arms at Cadiz, the Ile de Rhé, and La Rochelle. In those years also, the Palatinate remained unfreed, and the protestant forces in Europe under Mansfeld were defeated. A great many Englishmen, faced with the continued failure by James, Charles and Buckingham to assist Frederick with whole-hearted assistance at the right time and

[1] S. R. Gardiner, 'The Political Element in Massinger', *The Contemporary Review*, 1876, pp. 495–507.

[2] Particularly in the case of *The Maid of Honour*, in which Massinger carefully points to the dishonourableness of the military adventure which Gardiner's thesis makes Massinger approve of. See my 'Massinger the Censor' in *Essays on Shakespeare and Elizabethan Drama*, ed. R. Hosley, 1962, pp. 344–5.

in the right place, had the growing conviction that the causes both of Protestantism and of English national honour were being betrayed. The sense of affront in the attempts to raise the forced loan and in the shaming incompetence of English naval and military adventures made the mood of the newly assembled third parliament in the spring of 1628 one of the gravest concern for the preservation of England, of her national honour, and of the ancient rights of her people. It was the need to restore the past which was the burden of the speeches by Coke, Wentworth and Selden. 'The violated rights of the subject must first be vindicated. The very being of the commonwealth, they declared, was at stake.' So wrote Gardiner.[1] 'It is conceived,' said Sir Walter Erle, 'that the subject had suffered more in the violation of the ancient liberties within these few years than in the three hundred years before.'[2] Eliot's speech of 3 June made a strong contrast between England in the days of Elizabeth and England under Charles and Buckingham.

> What perfect English heart is not almost dissolved into sorrow for the truth? For the oppression of the subject . . . the whole kingdom is a proof. And for the exhausting of our treasures, that oppression speaks it. What waste of our provisions, what consumption of our ships, what destruction of our men have been! . . . We were never so much weakened, nor had less hope now to be restored. [3]

It must not be thought that the resentment was entirely a matter of principle: it was, for the merchants, a matter of money. The valiant merchant Richard Chambers exclaimed, 'Merchants are in no part of the world so screwed and wrung as they are in England. In Turkey they have more encouragement.'[4] For this, he was arrested and brought before the Star Chamber.

Charles eventually gave his assent to the Petition of Right, and

---

[1] S. R. Gardiner, *History of England 1603–1642*, 1884, VI, 231.
[2] Ibid., VI, 268.
[3] Ibid., VI, 300.
[4] Ibid., VII, 4, 84.

in August 1628 Buckingham was assassinated. But confrontation could not be avoided. By January and February, 1629, it had become clear that the issue was one of sovereignty: who was to govern England? 'Actum est de imperio'.[1] In March, 1629, Parliament was dissolved and Eliot and the eight members were imprisoned. Charles entered on the eleven-year-long career of his personal rule.

It is of the utmost importance to stress that nostalgia and reaction were basic elements in the opposition to Charles at the time that *Perkin Warbeck* and *Believe As You List* were written. The appeal voiced by Eliot, Wentworth and Selden was to the 'ancient rights' of the people. The complaint was not that Charles was a feudal incubus, hampering progress and the advancement of freedom, but that, in his autocracy and would-be absolutism, he was a dangerous innovator. Lawrence Stone's book, *The Causes of the English Revolution 1529–1642* (1972), clearly illustrates the basic conservatism of the early period of the English revolution and relates it to the profound and wide-spread reactionary element in revolutionary movements as a whole. (When the split came ten years later those M.P.s who took Parliament's side were on average ten years *older* than those who sided with the king.[2]) Those who opposed Charles wished not to advance but to return, and the reign of Queen Elizabeth took on a quite extraordinary sentimental lustre as the golden image of all that life under the Stuarts failed to be.[3]

In a situation of national humiliation, coupled with fear of the encroachment of a new kind of absolutism, and a tendency to look to the past for an image of what ought to be, it seems very natural to me that one of the strongest myths of mankind should be revived by Ford and Massinger, the myth of the hero who returns from the dead to succour his oppressed people.[4] The myth has attached itself to Arthur, to Harold, to James IV of Scotland, to Parnell. The Sebastian cult, interestingly, has been one of the most

[1] Ibid., vii, 63.

[2] Stone, *The Causes of the English Revolution*, p. 133.

[3] See C. V. Wedgwood, *Oliver Cromwell and the Elizabethan Inheritance*, Neale Lectures in English History, 1939.

[4] Cf. C. Hill, *Puritanism and Revolution*, 1965, p. 55.

long-lived versions of the myth of the 'sleeping hero': it manifested itself until the end of the nineteenth century.

> The plot in which the vine takes root
> Begins to dry from head to foot:
> The stock soon withering, want of sap
> Doth cause to quail the budding grape:
> But from the neighbouring elm, a dew
> Shall drop, and feed the plot anew.

So runs the oracle's riddle in Ford's *The Broken Heart*.

My main proposition, therefore, is that both Perkin Warbeck and Antiochus represent a luminous figure appearing from the mists announcing that he is the dead past, newly come alive in order to bring succour to an ailing nation. He has a kind of beauty of being, he is the guardian of the idealized, authentic, undivided life, when truth and government were not separated. It is a notable blend of romance and reality that in Massinger's play it is the merchants who are most obviously suffering under the Roman yoke, and long for the old régime (383–409; 494–511); it was the merchants who had the most to complain about over Charles's attempts to exact subsidies.

A charismatic figure of lost royalty would have had a great emotional appeal at a period when many of Charles's subjects looked on the occupant of the throne as the dried husk of a king. But we must renounce two things completely if we are to make sense of the conflict of the two 'competitors for kingdoms' (Ford's phrase) in each play. The first is the temptation to read the plays allegorically, and the second is the nineteenth-century view of Charles I as the pale figure of an obsolete Divine Right theorist holding up the cause of economic liberty. For if we don't renounce these things, it will appear ludicrously 'unhistorical' that the returning king-hero should suffer defeat at the hands of mercilessly efficient machiavellian statecraft. It may well be that a strong sense of national disgrace caused by an incompetent monarch triggered off the pretender plays. But as Henry VII or Philip II (in the original version) began to take shape in the dramatist's mind, he was not a mask for Charles I, but a metaphor for a kind of modernism which, however odd it seems, might have been thought to include the objects of Charles's policies.

Trevor-Roper's theory of the general crisis of the seventeenth century[1] recognizes as a fundamental element in the unease of Europe an alarm at the growth of the impersonal power of the Renaissance state. Absolutism belonged to the future in Europe,[2] and the fact that Charles was incompetent was no bar to feeling in his policies the merciless wind of change.

The machiavel, as the representative of unwanted progress and modernism, had haunted the imagination of English dramatists for fifty years. As he appears in these pretender plays, he seems bound for a highly successful future as he completes his task of eroding and replacing traditional human and social values. Both *Perkin Warbeck* and *Believe As You List* are very pessimistic plays, and they by no means share the confidence of Ralegh as expressed in the epigraph to this essay. We are invited to see in each play a spiritual hollow-ness in the established government, and to share a conviction that the ethics of success on which it builds are bound to suppress the qualities of truth represented by the saintly king beckoned up from the past.

In associating Massinger and Ford with a deep current of hostility to Charles, I have made it quite clear that their position is not anti-monarchical. Everyone was a monarchist in 1630 and dramatists were utterly dependent on the monarchy for the continuance of their profession. The force behind the pretender figure is the feeling that Charles was betraying the monarchy. But the time was rapidly passing when it was possible to represent the conflict as a competition between two kings. It seems to me a strangely prophetic stroke that in the enforced revision of his play Massinger had to exchange the kingdom of Spain for the republic of Rome, so that the ethos of modern expediency and progress became associated with republicanism. The year 1630 was about the time when many thoughtful people who had opposed Charles began to question their loyalties and ask whether their belief in

[1] H. R. Trevor-Roper, 'The General Crisis of the Seventeenth Century', in *Crisis in Europe 1560–1660*, ed. T. Aston, 1965, reprinted 1970, pp. 59–95.
[2] Stone, *op. cit.*, pp. 132–3.

what monarchy ought to stand for did not demand their support of the king. As Wentworth joined the King's service, he made his great speech at York, expressing his belief in 'those mutual intelligences of love and protection descending and loyalty ascending which should pass and be the entertainments between a king and his people'.[1] A young lawyer-friend of Massinger's, Henry Parker, made a different decision. He was the first person to propound a theory of the sovereignty of Parliament, and he wrote, 'Reason of state is something more sublime and imperiall than Law ... When warre has silenced Law ... Policy is to be observed as the only true Law.'[2] This is the language of Massinger's Flaminius, also agent of a republic. Twenty years after Massinger and Ford wrote their plays, the king had become the natural symbol of traditional relationships and 'ancient rights', and the vehicle for modernism and progress was the Commonwealth. In 1630, the simplicity of these divisions had not established themselves; in the theatre, the warfare in the soul of England could be best expressed as a contention between rival kings.

The exact circumstances in which Massinger and Ford came to write their pretender plays cannot be discerned. Though they were friends, the appearance of the two plays may be a coincidence. But the fact that the two plays exist side by side helps us considerably to see the force of each as a political play exploring the meaning of the terms 'counterfeit' and 'natural' in the period of perturbed and perplexed relationships between monarch and people about the year 1630.

[1] Gardiner, *History of England*, VII, 26.
[2] M. A. Judson, 'Henry Parker and the Theory of Parliamentary Sovereignty', *Essays in History and Political Thought in Honor of C. H. McIlwain*, 1936, p. 156.

The Artistry of 'Bleak House'

D. W. JEFFERSON

PERCY Lubbock's account of *Bleak House* is in some respects inaccurate and, as a piece of Dickens criticism, unsatisfactory by modern standards. But it also has some of the virtues that one would expect in such a connoisseur of narrative art, and even where it fails it may serve as a valuable point of departure for discussion. He begins with Stevenson's observation that

> ... Dickens's way of dealing with his romantic intrigues was, to lead gradually into them, through well-populated scenes of character and humour; so that his world is actual, its air familiar, by the time that his plot begins to thicken ... *Bleak House* is a very good case; the highly coloured climax in that book is approached with great skill and caution, all in his most masterly style. A broad stream of diversified life moves slowly in a certain direction, so deliberately at first that its scope, its spread, is much more evident than its movement. The book is a big survey of a quantity of odd and amusing people, and it is only by degrees that the discursive method is abandoned and the narrative brought to a point. Presently we are in the thick of the story, hurrying to the catastrophe, without having noticed at all, it may be, that our novel of manners has turned into a romantic drama, with a mysterious crime to crown it ...
>
> The world which he peopled with Skimpole and Guppy and the Bayham Badgers was a world that could easily include Lady Dedlock, for, although she is perhaps of the theatre, they are certainly not of the common earth. They and she alike are at the same angle to literal fact, they diverging one way, she another; they accordingly make a kind of reality which can assimilate her romance.[1]

[1] *The Craft of Fiction*, London (1921), pp. 213–14.

One cannot speak nowadays of Lady Dedlock's story as mere 'romantic drama'. Modern readers have learnt to see her cruel self-deprivation and denial of love, the misery of her lover's death and her own, as tragedy. But even if we agree with the modern critical emphasis on the moral seriousness of Dickens's art, we may also agree that he made the most of those elements that produce mystery and a heightening of atmosphere and tension. It could be claimed that *Bleak House* is more successful in its organization at this level of appeal than any of his other works. Considering the immense length of these novels we need not regard this as a trivial recommendation. Lubbock's phrase is inadequate rather than totally incorrect. The idiom of romantic drama is evident but is intensified by the moral theme.

The mental image that Lubbock presents is of a plot growing up through the centre of a novel that spreads also in other directions, and *Bleak House* is offered as a very good example of this pheno-menon. But is there another example of comparable merit? A similar effect is attempted in *Little Dorrit*, but unconvincingly. The curiosity, never very avid, created in us by the ominous 'dreams' of Mrs Affery is disappointed in the end by revelations that are tediously complicated. It is a static mystery—as static as Mrs Clennam, almost as much confined within her four walls as she is herself before her final act, and almost entirely barren of interest-ing involvements for the characters elsewhere, relevant to the history of the Dorrits though it proves to be. Dickens tries, using the monstrous, ubiquitous Blandois, to give the impression of an interrelatedness between different parts of the book, but the con-nections are a little faked. The greatness of *Little Dorrit* is beyond question, but it lacks a sufficiently animating plot: a plot that is central and implicates a large variety of characters in ways that keep action stirring. Dickens's success with the plot of *Bleak House*, on the other hand, will bear a good deal of examination. In Lubbock's words 'he leads gradually into [it]', and some routine details of its course may be of service here. In Chapter 2 Lady Dedlock receives a shock when she notices the handwriting on the law document. The first four chapters of Esther's narrative now follow, and these do not advance the plot. In Chapter 7 Mr Guppy, visiting Lady Dedlock's home, sees her portrait, and is struck by its likeness to somebody, and we are not told that it is to Esther, whom he was employed to look after on her first day in London (Chapter 4). But in Chapter 9, again in Esther's narrative, Mr Guppy makes his extraordinary proposal to Esther, referring obscurely to opportunities that, blest with her hand, he would have for advancing her interests. We leave Esther's narrative and in the next chapter Mr Tulkinghorn begins to follow up the business of the handwriting. With the help of Mr Snagsby he traces the writer, calls on his wretched lodging in Mr Krook's strange establishment, only to find that he has just died of an overdose of opium. The following chapter contains descriptions of the inquest and burial, and in the next Mr Tulkinghorn announces the disagreeable event in the presence of Lady Dedlock, who receives it with characteristic *sang froid*. But four chapters later (Esther's account of the Bayham Badgers, the Coavinses family, Gridley and the Turveydrops occupies the interval) there is a portentous development. Lady Dedlock, disguised as a servant, escapes from her imprisoned and exclusive existence and steps down to the dreadful slum where she finds the boy Jo who gave evidence at the inquest and who can show her the grave of the miserable law-writer. Jo is in demand in more than one quarter. In Chapter 19 he is telling the story of the strange lady in the home of Mr and Mrs Snagsby, with Guppy and the Chadbands paying attention. In Chapter 22 he is interrogated by Mr Bucket in Mr Tulkinghorn's chambers, and asked to identify the woman with 'the wale, the bonnet and the gownd' who appears to be and yet is not the lady of the earlier episode. The plot is still some distance from its peak but this fragmentary sketch may give some idea of the kind of plot that it is. It branches out, events are fruitful in consequences that concern an ever-increasing number of participants with interlocking interests. It abounds in scenes with surprising combinations of personages. There is continual movement, not only from situation to situation but also between a striking variety of settings: Chesney Wold, Tom-all-Alones, the Snagsbys' parlour, Mr Krook's junk-shop.

What Lubbock failed to note is that the plot, the Lady Dedlock story, belongs primarily to the 'impersonal' narrative (if the epithet can appropriately be applied to a voice that can sometimes be so impassioned), and that the gradualness of its progress is mainly due to its being interrupted by Esther Summerson's narrative. The plot stands still during her story in the early half of the book, largely because her part in the plot, her role as Lady Dedlock's child, is still unknown to her and remains so until the comparatively late stage when it becomes known to Lady Dedlock herself. Meanwhile Esther has found other roles and a world of associations quite unrelated to that in which her mother's destiny unfolds itself.

Although the novel has two narrative systems, the connections between them begin so soon that the reader always experiences them as one exceptionally rich whole. Mr Guppy's movements in the early chapters are an early example of what may be referred to as 'crossing over'. Mr Krook's house, the scene of Nemo's death, has already been the scene (in Chapter 5) of one of Esther's experiences: the visit, with Ada, Richard and Caddy, to Miss Flite's apartment. In Chapter 14 she pays her second visit, to learn of Miss Flite's illness after the tragedy, so that here her story specifically by-passes an event of supreme relevance to it.

There are, of course, big differences between the two structures: for example, in the way characters make their appearance and are related to each other. In the Lady Dedlock story characters are related to each other mainly through the plot. In Esther's narrative there is no plot and the organization is more relaxed: characters appear because they are hangers-on of Mr Jarndyce, or because Esther makes them her friends, or because Richard takes up a series of occupations, each with its professional representatives, like the Bayham Badgers. They are seen as acquaintances of Esther. Characters in the other narrative tend to be seen at a greater distance, in an elaborately composed context of situation and atmosphere. Their own reticence and the narrator's in scenes where there is mystery are in striking contrast to the openness of Esther and her fresh, uncomplicated, truly human dealings with people. There are fine strokes of art in places where characters from the other narrative move into the foreground of Esther's; and none is more interesting than that (in Chapter 31) where Jo, in his feverish state, mistakes Esther for the 'lady'. ('I won't go no more to the berryin' ground . . .') But the central example of 'crossing over' is the episode (Chapter 36) where Lady Dedlock, quite literally stepping over to Esther in the field where she is resting after her walk, makes herself known to her as her mother. (This is actually not her first appearance in Esther's narrative. They have seen and then met each other, and curiosity has been aroused on both sides; but now the movement is completed.) After this she can only 'go back'—return, that is, to a life in which Esther cannot accompany her, but also to the narration to which her history belongs. In Esther's narrative she will not be seen again alive. But it is of immeasurable value that in this one passage they should have the chance to establish their love for each other. The double narrative technique achieves great beauty here. It is only when she finds her way into Esther's story, it is only when she is with Esther, that Lady Dedlock can be herself. For a brief moment at the end of Chapter 29, where she first learns that she has a daughter, we see her overcome with feeling, so that we are not totally unprepared for the scene with Esther; but the complete abandonment of the life of disguise in that scene gives it great dramatic felicity.

Not all readers are satisfied with it. Robert Garis writes:

> Even by theatrical standards, Esther's feelings are completely unrealized in the language, with the result that flat assertions of a love which is both 'natural' and 'overflowing' would seem pharisaical if they, and the whole scene, did not impress us as completely empty. And, of course, one reason for this is not only that what Lady Dedlock confesses must be suitable for the chaste ear of Esther, but that both of the protagonists in this scene reflect Dickens's deep lack of interest in the moral imagination.[1]

Would such a reader as Mr Garis be equally dissatisfied with the undifferentiated expressions of Christian feeling, for example, in the passages where Esther tries to comfort the woman in the brick-maker's cottage? How far this lack of individualization, this 'unrealized' quality, as it is termed, and the somewhat conventional

[1] *The Dickens Theatre*, London (1965), p. 141.

content of the recorded utterances, really matter, is a crucial issue in the assessment of Dickens; and there is no doubt that a declining fastidiousness about those alleged shortcomings has been part of the recent movement of criticism in his favour. Modern readers are more likely to be impressed by his intense moral conviction and the heartfelt quality that can co-exist with the commonplace and the conventional. In this particular scene we need perhaps to accept certain limits. Lady Dedlock has made a dramatic escape from her moral isolation, but she is never to become known to us in an individual way; and it is to moral isolation and disguise that she returns. As for Esther, we never actually see her, and a lack of definition is inherent in Dickens's treatment of her character. To accept Esther we need to recognize her as the chosen and cherished vessel of the novelist himself, the bearer of his message as well as of the story he tells through her, and refrain from criticizing her for not being 'fully realized' in the George Eliot manner. And the whole drama of the book depends on the existence of moral and social conventions which none of the characters, nor the novelist himself, is moved to challenge, and which we must accept as part of the *donnée*. What passes between Lady Dedlock and Esther in this episode is valid and compelling, within this framework.

It is within Esther's narrative that the life-giving forces in the novel are most active. Esther's capacity for loving relationships is a life-giving force in more than one sense: she is the novelist's resource in bringing characters into play. His creativeness and hers are in happy analogy. Mr Jarndyce is the main pillar of the book, as Esther's guardian, the wise and charitable cousin of Richard, the generous and tactful benefactor of Miss Flite and the Coavinses family, the unfailing exponent of humane values and centre of rational opposition to the insanities of Chancery. But he has also been cast for the traditional role, comic in origin, of the patron of unworthy and ridiculous hangers-on—Mrs Jellyby, Mrs Pardiggle, Mr Skimpole. Structurally his dual function, and the presence of these frauds, is very valuable. When Mrs Pardiggle presses Esther and Ada to accompany her to the brickmaker's cottage, which they do without any intention of giving countenance to 'do-gooders', what they see excites their compassion, and after Mrs Pardiggle has done her worst and departed, they stay on and give their affection to the woman whose child has died. And Esther's befriending of Caddy Jellyby occurs in a similar situation, where the false do-gooder is seen as a menace and natural goodness comes into its own. Mr Jarndyce's tolerance of these people creates contexts in which Esther's good deeds come spontaneously as an antidote to a sham. And in this way Dickens's dislike of officious philanthropy is taken care of. On an entirely different principle, but also with the effect of contrast, Mr Skimpole's bland announcement of the death of Neckett (Chapter 15), and his whimsical performance on the piano, have the effect of putting the reader in a frame of mind very favourable to acts of charity.

Mr Jarndyce as a kind of universal provider, to the just and the unjust, is an effective conception in a novel of this scope, which needs centres for its diversified life; but sometimes we may find it hard to believe in such blindness to Skimpole in the man whose 'quick perception' as well as his 'sweet temper' at Caddy's wedding breakfast is noted by Esther (Chapter 30). Mr Allworthy in *Tom Jones* is in the same tradition, an even clearer case of a benefactor figure needed by the plot for a variety of purposes; but with his suave formalizing techniques Fielding is perhaps more successful than Dickens in establishing a kind of coherence. Not that consistency in characterization is as important as is usually assumed. What sort of person do we take Esther to be? On the one hand she is a younger version of Lady Dedlock, sometimes mistaken for her, and therefore presumably a distinguished beauty; but she is also 'Dame Durden', the unassuming 'little woman' who keeps house for Mr Jarndyce; and to this may be added the usual contradictions that must arise when a humble person is entrusted with the narrative powers of the novelist. To most readers the 'multi-purpose' character raises no problems, and is not detected as such, provided that there is some leading human quality sufficiently in evidence to establish a continuing identity. Mr Jarndyce and Esther are the constant generators of sympathy and goodness, they are the human embodiment of what Dickens had to offer as a counterpoise to the extreme misery of the *Bleak House* world. Such characters, common in his novels, have been much criticized in the past, but in our time readers are perhaps more likely to be impressed by the sheer power and stamina needed to generate what a big Dickens novel needs to keep it morally alive. Esther is at the heart of the book, a dear figure to her creator, and it is difficult to see how we can fail to accept her without being in some way alienated from the novelist's most important concerns. Esther and Mr Jarndyce are, of course, greatly overworked, but this is their *métier*. They represent qualities that will never fail and are always in demand.

Perhaps this is the moment for a digressive comment on Dickens's characters in general. Lubbock's reference to the 'odd and amusing people' of *Bleak House* is a painful reminder of the unsatisfactory state of Dickens criticism half a century ago. (But his description of the compositional relationship between Lady Dedlock and the more comic characters, in the last sentences of the passage quoted from *The Craft of Fiction*, is interesting.) A few years later E. M. Forster was to associate him most damagingly with the invention of 'flat' characters. But this question of Dickens's methods of characterization is still not adequately discussed. It may be suggested that he was especially good with characters who see themselves in a particular role, so that their speech and mannerisms are an enactment of their fantasies. These characters are sustained by their fantasies and enjoy elaborating them. Mr Skimpole, who does this with great inventiveness, might almost be described as 'self-delighting', dreadful though he is. Even those who have developed their role to impose on others, as Skimpole and Turvey-drop do, are so wedded to it that it has virtually become second nature. Their role is their life, or almost. What has happened is a process of self-distortion, which is very different from saying that Dickens the 'caricaturist' (an insulting word), observing mannerisms from outside, has produced a bold simplification. These people live from within, but they have learnt to live in accordance with a specious, drastically reduced conception of their human function, so that they can live off others. To say that 'they don't develop', in the sense used by Forster, is meaningless. Their very role involves a halting of development. But we do see them adapting their role to varying circumstances. When Mr Jarndyce

sees that Jo is desperately ill (Chapter 31) and turns to Mr Skimpole
with the words: 'What do you say, Harold?' his reply is: 'You had
better turn him out.' He hasn't forgotten all his medical knowledge, and this response is so crudely practical that some readers
might wonder whether his role has suddenly slipped and he has
become one of Forster's 'round' characters after all. But we would
do better perhaps to treat it as compatible with the conceit with
which he assumes that he can get away with anything. To turn to
a harmless character: Mrs Bayham Badger, with the full support of
her third husband, lives in fantasy on the memory of her two
earlier ones, and of herself in the roles afforded by each marriage
in turn. But she is no fool, and when it becomes apparent to her
that Richard is only half-hearted about his profession, she handles
the matter very competently (Chapter 17), always in the idiom of
her obsession:

> It was a maxim of Captain Swosser's . . . speaking in his figura-
> tive naval manner, that when you make pitch hot, you cannot
> make it too hot; and that if you only have to swab a plank, you
> should swab it as if Davy Jones were after you. It appears to me
> that this maxim is applicable to the medical, as well as to the
> nautical profession.

The favourite theme, if primarily an eccentric indulgence, is also a
social ploy, a means in this case of avoiding bluntness. Her husband's mild way of agreeing with her, always sharing her reverence
for his illustrious predecessors, would tend to give an atmosphere
of amenity to a slightly sticky occasion.

Dickens's readers in the past sometimes complained that he
spoilt his fabulous creations by making them do things in the end
that seemed to conflict with the conception hitherto maintained.
('Flatness' can often be the result of the reader's selective and self-
indulgent way of appropriating the Dickens creation!) Thus
Skimpole, after Mr Jarndyce has parted company with him, writes
a book maliciously attacking his character. If Dickens does this
rather crudely here, at least he is at pains to show that there is a
distinction between the man and his role. If circumstances change
sufficiently the role will be discarded.

Some characters are simply themselves, without self-conscious-
ness (Sir Leicester Dedlock, George Rouncewell), but others
cherish and cultivate themselves, with an artist's pleasure in the
effect. Mr Smallweed is not only old and crippled. He makes the
most of this image of infirmity, and his enjoyment of the pleasures
of extortion is that of a connoisseur, an actor, who has shaped his
style of ogreishness to suit his condition. But he is genuinely
incommoded by age, and uncontrollably exasperated by his
imbecile wife, whom he addresses with brimstone invectives that
combine rhetorical invention with real savagery. By no means a
character to be summed up in Forster's way. A character who does
perhaps lay himself open to the charge of flatness is Mr Vholes—an
effective creation, certainly, but it is a weakness in the later part
of the novel that Richard's Chancery obsession is unrealized in any
specific events, enquiries, discoveries, or other changes in the
situation that would have shown Mr Vholes in action. We always
see him in terms of the same general self-description to which he
reverts on all occasions.

To return to the double narrative: the variations of rhythm and
mood between Esther's story and the other narrative are among
the beauties of the novel. The extraordinary imaginative achievement of the first two chapters, with their images of stagnation and
grotesque waste of life, has been often enough praised by modern
critics. Equally good in its contrasting way is Esther's opening
stretch of narrative in Chapter 3, described as a 'superb unbroken
sweep'[1] by Q. D. Leavis, who is not one of those who find fault
with Esther. Bleak House opens with bad weather, and there is fog
in London when Esther first arrives there; but Chapter 6 in her
narrative begins with a cheerful description of the sunshine that
has come after the clearing of the fog, and of the delightful country-
side on the way from London to Mr Jarndyce's home, which she
and her friends reach after nightfall. The next chapter begins with
the words: 'While Esther sleeps, and while Esther wakes, it is still
wet weather in Lincolnshire', and we go back to the sodden

[1] F. R. and Q. D. Leavis, *Dickens the Novelist*, London (1970), p. 127. I take the
opportunity to record my general indebtedness to Mrs Leavis's essay on *Bleak
House*.

depression of Chapter 2. In Chapter 8, after this brief interlude, we are with Esther again, as she gets up before daylight, ready for work, gradually becoming aware, as day breaks, of the pleasant scene from her window. These are graces of narrative that should be spared the reductive process of thematic patterning.

The alternations between the two narrative worlds, and the existence of Esther in one of them, made it possible for Dickens to do something very formidable in the other. The two narrative systems provide two separate perspectives, and within one of them he could be relentless. With its succession of powerfully composed images of human deprivation and desolation *Bleak House* is perhaps the most terrible of Dickens's novels. Yet it also has a buoyancy that, for example, *Little Dorrit* lacks. One of the reviewers of *Bleak House* complained of Dickens's 'taste for nastiness . . . He has a marvellous liking for whatever is physically offensive. He gloats over mould, damp, rottenness and smells'.[1] Absurd though this criticism is, written at a time when the real squalor of London was much worse than anything a novelist would have been free to reveal, it serves to call our attention to the fact that this novel, of all Dickens's works, goes furthest in its descriptions of the physical environment in which so many wretched people lived and died. The episode in which Nemo is discovered dead in his miserable lodging is distressing, but it is exceeded in this respect by the passage in Chapter 11, where he is buried in 'the hemmed-in churchyard, pestiferous and obscene', the horror and moral disgrace of which provoke the narrator to an exclamatory outcry: 'Come night, come darkness, for you cannot come too soon, or stay too long, by such a place as this!' There are other places in the book where the shocked and protesting voice of the narrator is raised to an even higher pitch. It is one of its characteristic features, though much of the 'impersonal' narration in the early stages is conducted with an aloofness that matches that of Lady Dedlock and is appropriate to the description of her life of moral impene-trability and stasis. In Chapter 16 the graveyard is again the setting, and its squalor is now further enhanced for us partly by the impact

[1] Quoted by Philip Collins in *Dickens: the Critical Heritage*, London (1971), p. 296.

it makes on Lady Dedlock, and partly by the wry humour of Jo, who is inured to this environment:

> 'He was put there,' says Jo, holding to the bars and looking in.
> 'Where! Oh, what a scene of horror!'
> 'There!' says Jo, pointing. 'Over yinder. Among them piles of bones and close to that there kitchin winder! They put him wery nigh the top. They were obliged to stamp upon it to git it in. I could unkiver it for you with my broom, if the gate was open.'

And then he notices a rat, which he points to with some relish, but which the woman shrinks from, as she shrinks from Jo and from the whole unbearable scene. In a few moments she has given him his money and has gone. This is a tragic passage, not only because of the sordid facts of the burial place but because of her utter loathing and flight from it, her incapacity to break out of her frozen existence. Continuing with the same theme we may turn next to Chapter 22, where Mr Bucket, accompanied by Mr Snagsby, visits Tom-all-Alones, in search of Jo. Tom-all-Alones has been described before, but now we experience it with Mr Snagsby, as a place

> ... reeling with such smells and sights that he, who has lived in London all his life, can scarce believe his senses. Branching from this street and its heaps of ruins, are other streets and courts so infamous that Mr Snagsby sickens in body and mind ...

The contemporary documentation for this has been very effectively supplied by John Butt,[1] from whom we learn that questions relating to public health were as topical in 1850 and immediately afterwards as the Court of Chancery itself. We know about Dickens's public involvement with these matters. It is right that modern critics, such as John Lucas in his admirable book *The Melancholy Man*, should stress the magnitude of Dickens's moral commitment in exposing such horrors, and that criticism should have moved away from the approach embodied in such thin

[1] John Butt and Kathleen Tillotson, *Dickens at Work*, London (1957), pp. 177 ff.

phrases as Lubbock's 'romantic drama'. But it is possible to move too far away from a concern with the 'craft of fiction', and more could be said about the virtuosity with which Dickens gives fictional life to these themes of social disgrace. For those who especially value the documentation and its moral, his method has the effect of supplying yet more.

At the beginning of Chapter 57 there is a decisive and final 'crossing over', the consummation of the whole design, when Inspector Bucket moves into Esther's narrative, with his request for her co-operation in the search for Lady Dedlock. It comes with the suddenness of an awakening from sleep and the prospect of an all-night journey. And now her mother's story has become, in the fullest sense, her story, and Esther's narrative reaches its culmination in the agony of the pursuit and its ending. This part of the book is wonderful in all kinds of ways. The very presence of Bucket in the novel is a piece of drama. With him the police detective, a recent innovation to which the Dickens of *Household Words* gave serious attention,[1] makes his *début* in fiction (Chapter 22)—and with what a flourish! And here he is, operating his techniques in spectacular fashion. As an early example of a highly skilled police pursuit of a fugitive, it is a splendid contribution to fiction. But, much more significantly, this is for Esther an initiation and the completion of a role. Life for her has not been altogether sheltered, but now it falls to her lot to visit the places of squalor and misery which hitherto have not belonged to her story. We are conscious of an important shift in the narrative structure as the two worlds converge. And there is also a shift in the perspective as these places are seen with Esther's eyes and are part of her mental suffering:

> At length we stopped at the corner of a little slimy turning, which the wind from the river did not purify; and I saw my companion, by the light of his lantern, in conference with several men, who looked like a mixture of police and sailors. Against the mouldering wall by which they stood, there was a bill, on which I could discern the words FOUND DROWNED ... I remained quiet; but what I suffered in that dreadful spot I can never forget. And it still has the horror of a dream.

[1] See Philip Collins, *Dickens and Crime*, London (1965 ed.), pp. 204 ff.

She describes a man in 'long swollen sodden boots', who whispers to Mr Bucket, and they go down some steps to look at an object, which turns out not to be what had been feared. On they go, and again they are near the river, Bucket concentrating hard on every detail of what passes. He turns to follow a 'shadowy female figure' that had flitted past and then gazes into the 'profound pit of water, with a face that made my heart die within me'; and this moment, she says, has lived with her: the image of the woman, and 'a face, rising out of the dreaded water'.

Part of the journey is through more pleasant places, and is enlivened by Bucket's briskness and sociability...'talking and drinking and shaking hands at every bar and tap', playing the role that gives cover to the other role, usually very ebullient, but at one point confessing himself baffled. This is after they visit the brick-maker's cottage, when he seems to have lost the scent. But he sees the truth and changes direction, back to London and then to the home of the Snagsbys, where inquiries are conducted which are totally obscure to Esther. The end comes at the burial ground, and again there is a description of its horror. She sees

> ... heaps of dishonoured graves and stones, hemmed in by filthy houses, with a few dull lights in their windows, and on whose walls a thick humidity broke out like a disease. On the step at the gate, drenched in the fearful wet of such a place, which oozed and splashed down everywhere, I saw, with a cry of pity and horror, a woman lying—Jenny, the mother of the dead child.

But, of course, it isn't, and her companions, Bucket and Allen Woodcourt, are unable to convey to her that her mother, to elude pursuit, had changed clothes with the poor woman. They decide that Esther's hands should be the first to touch her: 'They have a higher right than ours.' So, still uncomprehending, she goes to the gates where the body lies, and makes the discovery. A force greater than repugnance has driven Lady Dedlock to seek this union with her lover in death. The pattern of convergences is completed when Esther, by finding her mother, also confronts the grave of her father amid the squalor and stench of the burial ground. Although Esther's narrative continues, to the final defeat of Richard and her own happiness with Allen, and the other narrative also has a chapter or so to go, this great moment at the end of Chapter 59 really brings the dynamic relationship between them to its conclusion, and makes the *raison d'être* of the twofold structure finally apparent. Dickens's achievement in *Bleak House* is surely one of the most impressive and original in the whole of narrative art.

IV

Douglas and Surrey: Translators of Virgil

PRISCILLA BAWCUTT

THERE were several attempts in the sixteenth century to translate the *Aeneid* into English verse, yet the most successful translators were also the earliest: Gavin Douglas and Henry Howard, Earl of Surrey. Surrey and Douglas have been coupled by literary historians almost as automatically, if not as frequently, as Surrey and Wyatt. Scholars have debated again and again the nature of Douglas's influence upon Surrey. I prefer here, however, to consider some of the stylistic differences between Douglas and Surrey, and the relation between their styles and their aims and methods as translators. In 1589 Abraham Fleming, apologizing for the inadequacies of his translation of the *Georgics*, asked his readers

> to beare with such shifts as they shall see vsed heere and there for the conueiance of the poets sense in plaine words applied to blunt capacities, considering the expositors drift to consist in deliuering a direct order of construction for the releefe of weake Grammatists, not in attempting by curious deuise and disposition to content courtly Humanists . . .

Douglas and Surrey, it seems to me, partly exemplify this contrast between the translator as teacher and expositor, aware of the needs of 'weake Grammatists', and the translator as courtly poet writing for those as well educated as himself. The distinction is clearly an over-simplification. It fails to take into account how different were the two poets' conceptions of stylistic excellence. It does not do justice to Douglas's real poetic merits. Nonetheless it may draw attention to an important difference between these two translators, which has been neglected in some critical estimates of their work.

Since neither poet is well known today, it seems best to provide a few facts. Both were noblemen. Douglas (?1475–1522), a younger son of the fifth earl of Angus, was a churchman, and towards the end of his life became bishop of Dunkeld. Surrey (?1517–47), the eldest son of Thomas Howard, later duke of Norfolk, was a courtier and soldier, who took part in Henry VIII's campaigns in France and Scotland. Both men were involved in politics; towards the end of their lives both were accused of treason. Douglas, however, died in exile in London, while Surrey was executed. Douglas finished his translation of the *Aeneid* on 22 July 1513, but it did not appear in print for another 40 years (London 1553). Several MSS of his *Eneados* are extant, the best being written by his own secretary, Matthew Geddes. The textual position is good— there is no evidence of major revision by Douglas or of serious corruption, apart from the Protestantism of the 1553 print. Surrey translated two books only: *Aeneid* II and IV. It is uncertain when he composed them, and in which order. Some scholars consider that Surrey was influenced by the Italian translators of Virgil, Nicolo Liburnio and Hippolito de Medici, and argue that book II at least must be later than 1539. Surrey's most recent editor, Emrys Jones, thinks, however, that they were 'comparatively early' works.[1] The text of Surrey's translation presents problems. Book II exists only in Tottel's print of 1557, but book IV exists in three versions (Tottel, 1557; the Day–Owen print of 1554; and MS Hargrave 205). These texts differ in numerous details, and scholars disagree as to which of them is nearest to Surrey's original. Douglas and Surrey contrast in another respect: the Prologues to the *Eneados* have much to say about Douglas's approach both to Virgil and to translation, but nothing survives to tell us of Surrey's views apart from the poems themselves.

Douglas and Surrey have in common one thing which could not be taken for granted in the first half of the sixteenth century. Both made not loose versions or paraphrases of the *Aeneid* but

[1] *Henry Howard, Earl of Surrey: Poems*, ed. E. Jones, Oxford, 1964, p. xx. Quotations from Surrey are taken from Jones's reprint of Tottel's text. Quotations from Douglas are taken from *Virgil's Aeneid Translated ... by Gavin Douglas*, ed. D. F. C. Coldwell, Scottish Text Society, 1957–64. Except when otherwise indicated, I have used H. R. Fairclough's text of the *Aeneid* (Loeb Classical Library, 1934–5).

translations based directly—not at secondhand—on the Latin original. Douglas suggests something of the novelty of this undertaking in his pithy criticisms of the way Caxton mutilated the *Aeneid*:

> Clepand it Virgill in Eneados,
> Quhilk that he says of Franch he dyd translait,
> It has na thing ado tharwith, God wait,
> Ne na mair lyke than the devill and Sanct Austyne.
> (1, Prol, 140–3)

He asserts his own fidelity to Virgil:

> Quha is attachit ontill a staik, we se,
> May go na ferthir bot wreil about that tre:
> Rycht so am I to Virgillis text ybund.
> (1, Prol, 297–9)

But 'Virgillis text' in the sixteenth century was rather different from that we read today. Editions of this time differ from modern editions in spelling and punctuation; they often omit or insert whole lines, and complete half-lines; they have numerous odd lexical variants. Yet both Douglas and Surrey were dependent on the text available in such editions—Surrey's is not known, Douglas seems to have used an edition published by Jodocus Badius Ascensius, probably that of 1501—and if we are to assess their skill as translators we must first take this into account. Recent editors of both poets have recognized this, yet it is still possible for readers who have access only to modern Virgils to think, quite erroneously, that one or other translator has blundered. This is particularly true of Douglas. Many comic mistranslations and barbarisms in the spelling of names can be shown to originate not in his ignorance but in the peculiarities of his Latin text. In book II, for instance, where modern editions read *Thessandrus* (261) Douglas's edition read *Thersandrus*; so too it had *Athamas* not *Acamas* (262), *nunquam* not *umquam* (331), and the half-line *stant circum* (767) was completed. One splendid 'howler' for which not Douglas but his Latin text is responsible occurs at VIII, 703, where Douglas appears to translate Virgil's *cum sanguineo* as 'with hir kynd cosyng' (VIII, xii, 72) because his text read *consanguineo*. Since I have discussed elsewhere[1] the bearings of Douglas's text of Virgil upon his own translation, I will give only one further illustration. In describing Dido at the hunt Virgil uses of her the phrase *cui pharetra ex auro* (IV, 138). Douglas seems to render this as 'Hyngand by hir syde the cays with arrowis grund' (IV, iv, 17), thus losing a Virgilian detail (*ex auro*) while inserting one of his own ('by hir syde'). In fact Douglas's edition at this point read not *ex auro* but *ex humero*; Douglas was making an accurate translation of a defective text. Surrey seems to have had the same reading since he too translates as 'Her quyver hung behinde her backe' (IV, 176). Later in book IV Surrey appears to translate Virgil's *ferte citi flammas, date tela, impellite remos!* (594) as 'Hast on, cast flame, set sayle and welde your owers!' (IV, 792). A recent editor[2] says that Surrey here omits Dido's *data tela*. But sixteenth-century editions often had the variant *date vela*, which is what Surrey's 'set sayle' appears to translate. In isolation such small blurs do not materially affect our judgement of Surrey's accuracy, yet they can have a cumulative effect. Sometimes they may distort aesthetic judgements, as when Emrys Jones says of Surrey's

> Troy yet had stand, and Priams towres so hie
>
> (II, 73)

that it 'misses the dramatic force of [Virgil's] apostrophe'. Modern editions usually read *Troiaque nunc staret, Priamique arx alta maneres* (56), but there has long been debate as to the correct form of this line (*staret* or *stares, maneres* or *maneret*?) and it seems pretty clear that Surrey had a text which here read *staret . . . maneret*. It is possible that closer study of these variants in the Latin might shed light on the vexed textual problem of Surrey's book IV.

Critics of Douglas and Surrey seem agreed on the most striking difference between them: 'Douglas is diffuse, Surrey terse.'[3] This

---

[1] 'Gavin Douglas and the Text of Virgil', *Transactions of the Edinburgh Bibliographical Society*, Vol. IV, part 6, 1973, 213–31.

[2] W. Tydeman in his *English Poetry 1400–1580*, 1970, p. 235.

[3] H. B. Lathrop, *Translations from the Classics into English from Caxton to Chapman 1477–1620*, Wisconsin Studies in Language and Literature, no. 35, 1933, p. 100.

judgement has been repeatedly voiced, and is undoubtedly accurate. If we use the crudest test of all, we find that Douglas uses far more lines than Surrey to translate the same amount of Virgil. *Aeneid* II has 804 lines; to translate it, Surrey takes 1068 lines, but Douglas 1462. *Aeneid* IV has 705 lines; to translate it, Surrey takes 943 lines, Douglas 1374. Surrey is undoubtedly a terse and economical translator. He almost invariably avoids those empty tags and phrases which had characterized even the best medieval verse and persisted long into the sixteenth century. This may seem something of a negative recommendation, but in this period it is a positive virtue. His practice contrasts with that of Douglas, who does not disdain the occasional 'I ges', 'but faill', 'al and sum', or 'schortlie to conclude'—their purpose being, as he disarmingly remarks, 'to lykly my ryme' (I, Prol, 124). Surrey uses very few metrical aids or line-fillers. Two he has in common with Douglas may have been used partly to give an archaic colouring to his verse. These are the use of *gan* to form the preterite of verbs—'And fyrst of all Timoetes gan advise' (II, 45)—and the *y*-prefix to form past participles—'Scarce was the statue to our tentes ybroughte' (II, 219). Surrey seems often to have set out to compress the content of a Virgilian hexameter into a line of his own verse:

> Whether of guile, or Troyes fate it would
> > (II, 48 = *Aeneid* II, 34)

> So diverse ranne the giddy peoples minde
> > (II, 53 = *Aeneid* II, 39)

> 'Whoso thou art, learn to forget the Grekes.
> Hencefourth be oures; and answere me with truth.
> > (II, 186–7 = *Aeneid* II, 148–9)

Such compression contrasts strikingly with Douglas, who makes four lines out of the last passage:

> 'Quhat evir thou art, beis mery and glad,
> Forȝet the Grekis that lost ar and away,
> From thens fordwart thou salbe owris, perfay.
> Bot schaw trewly this a thing I inquer.
> > (II, iii, 6–9)

Four lines for Virgil's two; this is a common ratio in Douglas, for whom the couplet often corresponds to a single hexameter. On the rare occasions when Douglas does achieve compression Surrey sometimes responds by incorporating such lines whole into his own version. Thus Douglas renders *Aeneid* II, 313 as

> Vpsprang the cry of men and trumpys blist
> (II, vi, 31)

and this re-appears in Surrey as

> Upsprang the crye of men and trompettes blast.
> (II, 399)

Surrey sought to emulate more than Virgil's brevity. He attempted to 'imitate' some of the more striking formal qualities of Virgil's poetry, and in this, as Emrys Jones has convincingly argued, may be regarded as 'the first English classical poet'. Surrey's innovatory choice of verse seems to me directly inspired by Virgil. I find it more plausible to regard his blank verse as modelled on Virgil's own unrhymed hexameters than on the *versi sciolti* of Virgil's Italian translators, although Surrey may have shared with them the usual humanistic reaction against rhyme as a medieval barbarism. I have already illustrated some of Surrey's attempts to match the contents of his verse-line closely to Virgil's hexameter. His occasional unfinished lines—'Imagine all the rest' (II, 85) = *disce omnis* (II, 66)—are surely no accident but deliberate emulation of the Virgilian half-lines they translate. Emrys Jones has shown how Surrey also attempted the more difficult feat of imitating Virgil's verse paragraphs. Surrey often followed the syntax and rhetorical patterns of Virgil closely, as in his translation of Aeneas's last sight of Creusa:

> ter conatus ibi collo dare bracchia circum;
> ter frustra comprensa manus effugit imago,
> par levibus ventis volucrique simillima somno.
> sic demum socios consumpta nocte reviso.
> (*Aeneid* II, 792–5)

Thrise raught I with mine arms t'accoll her neck,
Thrise did my handes vaine hold th'image escape,
Like nimble windes, and like the flieng dreame.
So night spent out, returne I to my feers.

                                        (II, 1054–7)

(Line 1055 shows how the search for compression sometimes leads to a confusing ambiguity of syntax.) Surrey's technique seems particularly well fitted for dealing with impassioned speeches, as in this from the scene where Anna finds Dido dying:

Sister, for this with craft did you me bourd?
The stak, the flame, the altars, bred they this?
What shal I first complaine, foresaken wight?
Lothest thou in death they sisters felowship?
Thou shouldst haue calld me to like destiny:
One wo, one sword, one houre mought end us both.

                          (IV, 900–05 = *Aeneid* IV, 675–9)

Anna's questions have almost the speed and urgency of the Latin. Surrey has sometimes followed Virgil in the placing of words within the line: 'Lothest thou in death', for instance, has the same initial position as *sprevisti moriens*. He keeps Virgil's emphatic repetition of *hoc* in the opening lines, but gives it an idiomatic English form: 'for this . . . bred they this'. In lines 901 and 905 Surrey heightens the declamatory effect, and introduces rhetorical patterns which although appropriate have no strict parallel in Virgil. Douglas—as so often when he is rendering the big set speeches—is neither so neat nor so dramatic. Only at the close of the speech does Douglas excel in conveying the tenderness that lies behind Anna's reproaches:

This sayand, the hie bing ascendis onane,
And gan embrays half ded hir systir germane,
Culȝeand in hir bosum, and murnand ay,
And with hir wympil wipyt the blude away.

                                        (IV, xii, 85–8)

Surrey at this point sounds cold and feelingless:

> With wailefull plaint, whom in her lap she layd,
> The blak swart gore wiping dry with her clothes.
>
> (IV, 915–16)

The Prologues to the *Eneados* show that Douglas was not blind to the formal beauties of the *Aeneid*, which he often discusses and sums up in the key-term, 'eloquence'. He repeatedly disclaims the power to convey this 'eloquence' adequately:

> Quha may thy versis follow in all degre
> In bewtie, sentence and in grauite?
>
> (I, Prol, 53–4)

It is rare for Douglas to model his style closely on that of Virgil—the two most obvious exceptions are when Virgil uses alliteration or the figure of *repetitio*, both of which were congenial to Douglas. It seems indeed that Douglas felt freer to imitate Virgil in his original poems (such as Prologue XII) than in the translation.

Douglas was rarely a stylistic innovator. It is characteristic that Surrey chose as his medium the 'strange metre' of blank verse, whereas Douglas chose the decasyllabic couplet, a form long established as suitable for narrative and hallowed by the use of Chaucer. So too with his choice of language and phrasing: wherever possible, Douglas assimilated Virgil to narrative styles already existing in English rather than attempting to create a new style owing much to that of Virgil. One of the most distinctive strands in this composite tradition was the alliterative and often highly formulaic style that Douglas used for Virgil's battle scenes in the latter books of the *Aeneid*; poems like the *Wallace* furnished him with the native equivalent of an epic diction. Another strand was the courtly and romantic style associated with *The Knight's Tale* and *Troilus and Criseyde*. There are reminiscences of Chaucer throughout book IV, particularly in the description of Dido at the hunt:

> And scho at last of palyce yschit owt,
> With huge menȝe walking hir abowt,

Lappyt in a brusyt mantill of Sydony,
With gold and perle the bordour al bewry . . .
The goldyn button claspyt hir purpour weid.

(IV, iv, 13ff.)

Much in Douglas's literary inheritance predisposed him to a
leisurely and ample style of translation. It is clear also that his own
predilections as a poet were all towards the amassing of detail and
what he called 'fowth of langage' (I, Prol, 120), that fullness of style
which may have been influenced by humanistic praises of *copia* but
owed its theoretic justification largely to medieval rhetoric.
Although Douglas paid tribute to Virgil's poetic economy—'with
nevir a word invane' (I, Prol, 30)—he was perhaps more heartfelt
when he praised his 'copious fouth or plenitud' (I, Prol, 58).

But Douglas aimed at 'fouth' in another sense: that of complete-
ness. Surrey gave his readers only a sample of the *Aeneid*, and
selected what are probably its best-known and best-loved books.
Other poet-translators before and after him—editors too—have
shown the same preference; and poets close to him in time (Du
Bellay, Liburnio, Piccolomni, and Fanshawe) clearly felt the
same special fondness for book IV. Douglas, however, like Dryden,
took on his shoulders the weight of the whole *Aeneid* if not of the
'whole author', something that no other translator into English
was to achieve until a century later. Surrey seems to have responded
to the challenge of tackling Virgil in those books where his artistry
was most subtle and accomplished. Douglas was concerned, however, to preserve the integrity and the proportions of the *Aeneid*. In
Prologue I he speaks of this quite explicitly—one of Caxton's most
grievous crimes was to give a misleading prominence to the story
of Dido.

The scholar in Douglas also attempted to give his readers a taste
of the Virgilian scholarship that was normally available only to
'clerkis' who read Latin. Many things in his *Eneados* that might
seem extraneous are closely related to the contents and apparatus
of the Latin Virgils. One small example of this is the set of couplets
describing 'the Contentis of Euery Buke following' (vol. II, p. 18).
These are not Douglas's invention, but translate the *monosticha*

argumenta, 12 one-line summaries of the different books of the *Aeneid,* which commonly accompanied it in contemporary editions. Douglas modelled his 'wlgar' or vernacular Virgil on the Latin editions in many other respects. He translated the so-called 13th book, written by the Italian humanist, Maphaeus Vegius, not out of perversity but more in the spirit with which Everest is said to have been climbed—'because it was there', a regular supplement to the *Aeneid* in almost all editions of Virgil from 1471 to the middle of the seventeenth century. So too the marginal 'comment' that accompanies Douglas's book I deals with the same range of topics as is found in the commentaries of Servius and Ascensius, and is indeed often directly indebted to them. Even Douglas's moralizing Fourth Prologue, with its reflections on the 'fors' of love, its attack on the 'subtell wilis' of lust, and its allusion to St Augustine weeping over Dido, has its counterpart in Ascensius's introduction to book IV:

> describit poeta vim amoris . . . Id autem facit prudens et com-
> modus poeta quo mortales animos ab amorum illecrebis auertat
> cum nemo sit a Venereis laqueis tutus, nisi qui omne obiectum
> procul habuerit et carnis luxum domuerit . . .

Douglas's zeal as scholar and teacher had important conse-
quences for his translation. It affected his style in various ways, and was often directly responsible for his diffuseness. Much that seems at first sight interpolation or 'tiresome verbosity' is in reality an attempt to catch the fullness of Virgil's meaning—what Douglas calls his 'sentence'—and convey this to a relatively unsophisticated audience. Douglas is quite explicit as to his methods, and aware that it may lengthen his translation:

> Sum tyme the text mon haue ane expositioun,
> Sum tyme the collour will caus a litill additioun,
> And sum tyme of a word I mon mak thre,
> In witnes of this term "oppetere".
>
> (I, Prol, 347–50)

Consistently enough—if misguidedly—when Virgil used *oppetere* (as at *Aeneid* I, 96) Douglas translated it as 'Deit . . . bitand the erd'

(I, iii, 6), following Servius's explanation as *ore terram petere*. A word's etymology, real or fanciful, was a recognized part of its 'sentence'. Douglas himself shows how this concern with 'expositioun' was rooted in the teaching of the schools:

> Ane other proffit of our buke I mark,
> That it salbe reput a neidfull wark
> To thame wald Virgill to childryn expone . . .
> Thank me tharfor, masteris of grammar sculys,
> Quhar ȝe syt techand on ȝour benkis and stulys.
>
> (*Directioun*, 41 ff; vol. IV, p. 189)

(Perhaps Surrey first encountered Douglas's *Eneados* in this way, as a teaching aid. Douglas seems to have envisaged youthful noblemen as his main readers.)

If we examine Douglas's *Eneados* closely, it sometimes gives the impression of being translation and running commentary, all in one. Words, phrases, and even whole lines, that have no equivalent in Virgil often derive from the explanatory glosses of Servius and Ascensius. For some of these we can still see the need today: the identifying of Virgilian place-names as wood or mountain, sea or lake—'that horribill mont, Cawcasus hait' (IV, vii, 9) or 'the wod Hyrcany' (IV, vii, 12); the unravelling of patronymics—Virgil's *Atridae* (II, 104) becomes 'Agamenon als, and Menalay' (II, ii, 83); the explanation of the role of Vesta as 'goddes of the erth and fyre' (II, v, 91), or the nature of Avernus, 'Quhilk lowch is situate at the mowth of hell' (IV, ix, 82). What we may find more surprising is the need Douglas feels to elucidate words or phrases that seem comparatively straightforward. Where Virgil tells us that Palamedes was slain (*neci*, II, 85), Douglas tells us that he was 'stanyt to ded' (II, ii, 47). Where Virgil describes Sinon as *turbatus* and *pavitans* (II, 67 and 107), Douglas takes pains to stress Sinon's dissimulation, and renders as '*semyng* ful rad' and 'quakand . . . *as it had bene* for dreid' (II, ii, 18 and 88). Even an adverb like *tandem* (IV, 304) has its contextual implications brought out in 'at the last . . . Eftir lang musyng' (IV, vi, 47–8). In each case Douglas followed the hint of a commentator—Servius had glossed *neci* as *lapidibus interemptus est*, and had also commented on Sinon: *quasi turbatus* and *quasi pavitans*. Ascensius had glossed *tandem* as *post longam cogitationem*. Douglas had a purpose similar to the commentators—to draw out the underlying 'sentence', even of the smallest word. One of the effects is to make Virgil's hints and ambiguities clear and definite, to turn the implicit into the explicit. Thus at IV, 448 Virgil does not specify what emotion Aeneas felt after Anna had pleaded with him: *magno persentit pectore curas*. But Douglas tells us precisely what the *curas* were—'of reuth and amouris felt the perturbance' (IV, viii, 85)—probably because he had read Ascensius's gloss: *idest sollicitudines amoris et miserationis*.

Surrey also consulted the commentators at times. He translated *agmina conscia iungunt* (II, 267), for instance, as 'They joyne them selves with the conjured bandes' (II, 339). Surrey's use of 'conjured' here has been thought to betray the influence of Hippolito's Italian rendering, *coniurate*. It seems more likely that both translators at this point were adopting Servius's gloss on *conscia*: *coniurata*. Like Douglas Surrey sometimes simplified Virgil's rich allusiveness; like Douglas he sometimes found the hints of the commentators helpful. Thus he translated Dido's words

> non ego cum Danais Troianam exscindere gentem
> Aulide iuravi classemve ad Pergama misi.
>
> (IV, 425–6)

as

> I with the *Grekes* within the *port Aulide*
> *Conjured* not the Troyans to destroy
> Nor to the *walles of Troy* yet sent my fleete.
>
> (IV, 557–9)

We do not need to posit the influence of Liburnio on the italicized words, when in numerous editions of Virgil Surrey could have read this note of Ascensius:

> ego non iuraui. idest *coniuraui* cum Danais. idest *Graecis*. Aulide pro Aulidi. idest in illo *portu* Euboici sinus . . . vel ego non misi classem ad pergama. idest *moenia Troiana*.

Surrey did not disdain the help of the commentators. But he was far more selective than Douglas in this as in other respects. He adopted a gloss chiefly to simplify or clarify the sense; only rarely did he add the explanatory detail so common in Douglas. He never, I think, followed the commentators in their practice of multiple glossing, a pedagogic habit, which had a marked effect on Douglas's style. It reinforced Douglas's taste for heaping up near-synonyms, and often led to a kind of 'double translation' already illustrated in his rendering of *tandem*, and evident also in the following:

> spoliis se quisque *recentibus* armat
> (II, 395)

> Ful glaidly in that *recent* spulȝe *warm*
> Belyf ilk man dyd thame self enarm.
> (II, vii, 59–60)

Contrast Surrey's

> The whole youth gan them clad in the *new* spoiles.
> (II, 505)

> ilicet obruimur *numero*.
> (II, 424)

> By *multitude and nowmyr* apon ws set
> All ȝeid to wraik.
> (II, vii, 109–10)

Cf. Ascensius on *numero*: *idest multitudine ingruentium.* Contrast Surrey's

> We went to wreck, with *nomber* overlayd.
> (II, 542)

> *hauriat* hunc oculis ignem crudelis ab alto
> Dardanus.
> (IV, 661–2)

Now lat ʒon cruel Troiane *swelly and se*
This our fyre funerale from the deip see.

(ɪv, xii, 35–6)

Contrast Surrey's

And from the seas the cruel Troyans eyes
Shal wel *discern* this flame.

(ɪv, 882–3)

Here and elsewhere Douglas in his anxiety to convey Virgil's
'fouth' of meaning sometimes gives us both the Latin word and
then a native equivalent (so too *facilis* becomes 'facil and eith', and
gubernaclum 'helmstok or gubernakill of tre'); sometimes Virgil's
own word (or one etymologically close to it) is paired with another
Latinate word derived from the commentators; sometimes he
tries, rather clumsily, to convey both the literal and the figurative
aspects of a Virgilian metaphor. These passages do not show
Douglas at his most felicitous, but they show him struggling with
the implications of Virgil's language in a way that is less true
perhaps of Surrey.

I will end by examining what Douglas and Surrey make of a
fine passage in *Aeneid* ɪɪ, the scene where Aeneas sees for the first
time battle raging in Troy:

excutior somno et summi fastigia tecti
ascensu supero atque arrectis auribus adsto:
in segetem veluti cum flamma furentibus Austris
incidit, aut rapidus montano flumine torrens
sternit agros, sternit sata laeta boumque labores
praecipitesque trahit silvas; stupet inscius alto
accipiens sonitum saxi de vertice pastor.

(ɪɪ, 302–8)

Affrayit, I glystnyt of sleip and start on feit,
Syne to the howssis hed ascendis onone,
With eris prest stude thar als stil as stone.
A sownd or swowch I hard thar at the last,
Lyke quhen the fyre be fellon wyndis blast

Is drevyn amyd the flat of cornys rank,
Or quhen the burn on spait hurlys down the bank,
Owder throu a watir brek or spait of flude,
Ryvand vp rede erd as it war wod,
Down dyngand cornys, all the pleuch laubour atanys,
And dryvis on swyftly stokkis, treis and stanys:
The sylly hyrd, seand this grysly syght,
Set on a pynnakill of sum cragis hycht
Al abasit, nocht knawand quhat this may meyn,
Wondris of the sovnd and ferly at he has seyn.

(II, vi, 8–22)

I waked; therwith to the house top I clambe,
And harkning stood I: like as when the flame
Lightes in the corne by drift of boisteous winde,
Or the swift stream that driveth from the hill
Rootes up the feldes and presseth the ripe corne
And plowed ground, and overwhelmes the grove,
The silly herdman all astonnied standes,
From the hye rock while he doth here the sound.

(II, 386–93)

We see here some of Douglas's weaknesses—the redundant 'onone' and 'at the last'; the conventional but more meaningful 'as it war wod', here serving chiefly 'to lykly the ryme'; the threefold explanation of *inscius* as 'sylly', 'abasit' and 'nocht knawand quhat this may meyn'. We may contrast with this the taut economy of Surrey—there are few superfluous words. Surrey often follows Virgil in the emphatic placing of significant words: 'I waked', 'Lightes', and 'Rootes up' all are first in the line, corresponding to Virgil's *excutior, incidit,* and *sternit.* Yet despite Douglas's diffuseness I find his translation more successful. Surrey's 'harkning stood I' is accurate but colourless as a translation of Virgil's *arrectis auribus adsto.* Douglas is more faithful to Virgil's 'sentence' in showing Aeneas tense and straining his senses to hear: 'With eris prest stude that als stil as stone'. In the two similes Virgil uses forceful verbs and adjectives: *furentibus, incidit, praecipites, trahit.* Apart from 'boisteous' and 'Rootes up', Surrey's choice of diction is sometimes tamely abstract—'overwhelmes the grove'—and sometimes distinctly lacking in energy—'Lightes in the corne by drift'. Douglas conveys the speed and the destructiveness of first the fire and then the flood. He was prepared to range more widely in the vocabulary than Surrey, and the words he chooses are down to earth, apt and forceful: 'fellon ... blast', 'hurlys', 'Ryvand', 'dyngand'. To some extent he recreated the second image, adding a visual detail ('rede erd') and breaking up *siluas* into small particulars: 'stokkis, treis and stanys'. Not unfittingly, he has transposed Virgil's *rapidus torrens* into a Scottish 'burn on spait'.

It is difficult in a short space to characterize these two translators adequately. Each has weaknesses which seem inextricably related to their strengths. Surrey rivals Virgil in terseness and sometimes in elegance of phrasing, but only rarely matches the richness and suggestiveness of his language. Douglas has nothing of Virgil's economy, and can be pedantic and over-explicit when the expositor in him destroys the poet. But he is far more responsive than Surrey to Virgil's linguistic subtlety. At his best Surrey mirrors in his own work the polished surface of Virgil. Douglas, at his best, penetrates beneath the surface and conveys something of Virgil's mysterious latencies of feeling:

> I haue translait a volum wondirfull:
> So profund was this wark at I haue said,
> Me semyt oft throw the deip sey to waid;
> And sa mysty vmquhile this poecy
> My spreit was reft half deill in extasy.
>
> (*Directioun*, 102–6; vol. IV, p. 190)

V

Crazy Jane and 'Byzantium'

NICHOLAS BROOKE

IT IS impossible to discuss Yeats without mentioning both 'Byzantium' and Crazy Jane; but it seems, to judge from my own experience (both as reader[1] and speaker), very nearly as impossible to mention them both in the same breath. They are diverse, sheer opposites. But they are also contemporaneous, since both were printed in different parts of *The Winding Stair* in 1932–3. 'Byzantium' is a climactic poem in the first part, and the seven Crazy Jane poems open the second part, 'Words for Music Perhaps'. They are not, therefore, adjacent; there are several short poems in between and one longer one, 'Vacillation', where Heart triumphs in a dialogue with Soul and announces original sin as its chosen theme. Original sin is certainly the theme of Crazy Jane; or rather, Crazy

---

[1] There have been numerous exegeses of 'Byzantium' which helps to economize my explanations; but they cannot be evaded because there is not general agreement. Two which I have most in mind are: G. S. Fraser, 'Yeats' "Byzantium",' *Critical Quarterly* (1960) and Denis Donoghue: *Yeats* (Fontana Modern Masters 1971). Crazy Jane is often alluded to and sometimes quoted, but rarely discussed; and when she has been more closely examined it has not been with unqualified admiration. The fullest and most illuminating essay is Denis Donoghue, 'The Vigour of its Blood: Yeats's "Words for Music Perhaps",' *Kenyon Review* (1959); Donoghue recognized that she was defiantly partial, but sought in vain for a unifying image, and reproved her sexuality (as perhaps most of us would have done in 1959) by comparison with *Lady Chatterley's Lover*. B. Rajan, in his sensitive and perceptive *W. B. Yeats: A Critical Introduction* (1965), referred to 'obvious anatomical puns' and 'much-vaunted sexuality' without apparent enthusiasm, and rather over-stressed her 'whole Body and soul' in a similar search for unity. Fraser likewise found a lack of final reconciliation in 'Byzantium'. It will be obvious that I could not have written this essay without a knowledge of Yeats's *A Vision*, but I have avoided direct reference since the poems are independent entities and not mere illustrations of the system. I discovered that the Crazy Jane poems were more obscure than they seemed a few years ago from the promptings of students in a seminar, and I should acknowledge my debt to them, to subsequent classes and lecture audiences, and to my wife.

Jane *is* original sin. 'Byzantium', on the other hand, is very obviously to do with 'soul' as distinct from 'heart'. So the sequence of poems as Yeats arranged it—'Byzantium' ... 'Vacillation' ... Crazy Jane—does suggest a relationship, and that is what Yeats implied in his characteristically half-oracular, half disarmingly simple dedicatory letter to Dulac:

> Then in the spring of 1929 life returned as an impression of the uncontrollable energy and daring of the great creators; it seemed that but for journalism and criticism, all that evasion and explanation, the world would be torn to pieces. I wrote 'Mad as the Mist and Snow', a mechanical little song, and after that almost all that group of poems called in memory of those exultant weeks 'Words for Music Perhaps'. Then ill again, I warmed myself back into life with 'Byzantium' and 'Veronica's Napkin', looking for a theme that might befit my years.

The chronological order explained here is reversed in the published volume so that 'Byzantium' appears before Crazy Jane with 'Vacillation' (dated two years later) in between them. The rather cryptic reference to 'a theme that might befit my years' can hardly mean original sin, nor Crazy Jane who celebrates it. The search for such a theme in 'Byzantium' is evidently the search for an escape from 'The fury and the mire of human veins'.

But the search for a theme is not necessarily the finding of it, and reversing the order of these poems gives to that cryptic note the ironic twist that the theme found appears to be the opposite of the one searched for.

To begin with, then, the poems are offered as opposite ends of the scale which runs from soul to heart:

> The unpurged images of day recede;
> The Emperor's drunken soldiery are abed;
> Night resonance recedes, night-walkers' song
> After great cathedral gong;
> A starlit or a moonlit dome disdains
> All that man is,
> All mere complexities,
> The fury and the mire of human veins.

The last line, or rather the last three lines which lead in crescendo
to the last line, establish the rejection as a vehement shock, a very
powerful image of revulsion. In a sense the revulsion follows from
the loaded selection of humanity offered, but it is pressed irrefu-
tably, after the resonance of gong and dome, into the absolute '*All*
that man is*'*, and the scorn of 'All *mere* complexities', which leaves
nothing but 'The fury and the mire'. Only the most feeble of
special pleading can deny that that is the universal condition of
human veins. The intensity re-inforces the image of the starlit or
moonlit dome, and from that the poem can proceed.

Crazy Jane is a different proposition, take her where you will—
as, of course, you may.

> 'Love is all
> Unsatisfied
> That cannot take the whole
> Body and soul';
> *And that is what Jane said.*

The difference from 'Byzantium' is extreme: the light ballad tone
and the witty ironic refrains are remote indeed from the monumental splendours of the holy city. The image it sets up is equally
unlike, or rather it is displayed in an opposite way: there, we are
repelled from the attractions of sexuality; here, Jane, a sour old hag
as remote as possible from the obviously attractive, is *displayed*
most attractively.

The opening stanza assesses its point in the sexual weight of
'Unsatisfied', and in the pun on 'whole'/'hole' which locates the
soul absolutely within the body. The second and third stanzas
proceed to make clear how difficult the cliché is in experience: the
acceptance demanded by 'take the whole' is not the simple one of a
renaissance Venus, it involves 'Take the sour/If you take me', the
obvious joke of stanza 2. But it involves also the more difficult
problems of 'soul' represented in stanza 3 in terms very reminiscent
of Blake, the hidden shame of the transition from Innocence to
Experience: 'Naked I lay . . . Naked and hidden away', and that,
too, is what Jane said. Rather more surprisingly, though it would

be foolish not to see that the experience of shame contributes to the sourness before, as much as the disturbing 'naked and hidden away' leads forward to the longing for 'What can be shown', the unhidden nakedness sought in 'What true love be?' So Jane contemplates the day of judgement, not as moral denunciation, but as total revelation free of time—which invites the last refrain ' "*That's certainly the case*," *said he*', the timely reminder that all she and he stand for is here today and gone tomorrow.

That is also a timely recall of the poem to its proper tone, from which my comments may have seemed in danger of wandering too far. But to see how far it does go without destroying itself helps to understand the quality of the first stanza. The truth is that the isolation of 'Unsatisfied' in line 2 forces its simplest sexual sense against any concept of Platonic (or 'soulful') love to which, in her second song, Jane had retorted '*Fol de rol*'. But if that is the obvious stress in 'Unsatisfied', then it needs to be adjusted into the equal stress of 'Body and soul'. The stress moves from one to the other, or rather, because it never ceases to be ambiguous, traffics to and fro between the two. And that is what I have been trying to say about the poem as a whole, and especially about the consequence of the final refrain.

'Byzantium' on the other hand, *seems* to move decisively from body towards soul, or from time towards timelessness. In the second stanza the gravity is maintained, but there is also a striking contrast, for this has nothing of the monumental in utterance, structure or image. And yet it is in the end no less rhetorical; in fact 'I hail the superhuman' is the most blatantly rhetorical gesture in the poem. But its blatancy is set against a tone of dry abstract pursuit of a conceptual idea:

> Before me floats an image, man or shade,
> Shade more than man, more image than a shade;

The movement is intellectual, remote from the concreteness of stanza 1; the image here floats so vaguely that it has as yet no definition at all. The idea is evidently complex, but presumably not a *mere* complexity. The movement seems at first to be Man-Shade-Image, but it emerges that the Image exists *between* the man and the shade.[1] It is not a man, because it is free of mere complexities; nor is it a mere shadow. But this image is certainly not identified by any of the specific images which immediately follow:

> For Hades' bobbin bound in mummy-cloth
> May unwind the winding path;

Bobbin, mummy, and winding path give way to each other too rapidly and with too little individual definition for any of them to fulfil the strong concept of 'image' established in the opening lines; rather, they seem to sustain the dealing in conceptual ideas, meta-phors for exposition more than for contemplation; they all, successively, establish the idea of winding on as well as off, of going both ways. Yet, however transitory as images in themselves, they do suggest the pressure for concrete particulars to take over from abstract concepts, and the strenuous effort of the poem is thus directed towards the establishing of the elusive image itself.

That is even more apparent in what follows:

> A mouth that has no moisture and no breath
> Breathless mouths may summon;

The summoning a mouth can do is possibly 'calling' ('I hail . . .'), but the insistence on 'mouth' and 'mouths' sustains the movement towards concreteness, and suggests something more sensual, the summoning attraction to a kiss. In *The Only Jealousy of Emer* the Woman of the Sidhe, beyond death, 'summons' the ghost of Cuchulain, not quite dead, to a kiss which will finally divorce him from life, and at the same time satisfy her—but he draws back at the last moment. Such a kiss involves an interaction between living and not-living worlds: a mouth that has no moisture and no breath is certainly not living; a breathless mouth may be the same, or it may be a very living one, 'breathless' because panting with eagerness. The syntax is equally ambiguous: which mouth summons which can never be determined; or rather, it must be

[1] Fraser is helpful on the possible meanings of 'shade', from 'ghost' to 'shadow'.

seen as continually shifting while you regard it, like some forms of
optical illusion, from one to another and back again. The double
motion is recognized at the end of the stanza:

> I hail the superhuman;
> I call it death-in-life and life-in-death.

It is clear that it must be both ways round, and it is also clear that
this remarkably abstract language must prelude a more concrete,
sensual, image. This is a stanza of shadows, but it establishes a sense
of moving back and forth between shade and man, between
abstract and concrete; between, perhaps, soul and body, body and
soul: a trafficking without which either will become meaningless.

The difference between that and the traffic in Crazy Jane can,
perhaps, be shown most clearly in the first of the 'Words for
Music Perhaps', 'Crazy Jane and the Bishop', for it begins at the
same moment as 'Byzantium', at midnight, but moves in a very
different direction:

> Bring me to the blasted oak
> That I, midnight upon the stroke,
> (*All find safety in the tomb*)
> May call down curses on his head
> Because of my dear Jack that's dead.
> Coxcomb was the least he said:
> *The solid man and the coxcomb.*

Jane apparently moves decisively from Bishop to Jack, but her
mind still travels between them. She could not curse one half so
well if there were not a Bishop to curse—and clearly it was he (an
old book in his fist) who taught her how to do it. They change
places in the second refrain.[1] In stanza I the equation is simple:
the Bishop is a 'solid man' (a reliable establishment figure) and Jack
is plainly a coxcomb. But in the second stanza the Bishop is
both: still solid in his views, but a coxcomb in his shrill resentful

---

[1] See J. Unterecker: *A Reader's Guide to W. B. Yeats* (1959), p. 226. Unterecker
has useful notes on some of the other songs as well, though I do not find his
narrative interpretation convincing.

impotence: 'Cried that we lived like beast and beast'. In stanza 3 it is Jack who is both, a coxcomb still, but solid in a phallic sense:

> But a birch-tree stood my Jack:
> *The solid man and the coxcomb.*

In the last stanza it is Jack who, returning even as a ghost, is solidly reliable, and the Bishop who is a mere coxcomb. It has become again a question of which is man, which shade, and Jane herself is a very powerful image between them.

The other refrain—*All find safety in the tomb*—plays around in a similar though less specific way. In the second stanza it affirms that Jack is safe from the Bishop in the tomb, but in the third, as the Bishop's deformities emerge, it is he that begins to need safety when a mere cassock can no longer hide his backward tumescence in contrast to the erection which Jack so proudly displays. So, in the last stanza, 'safety' is not what Jack is seeking, and he wanders still, ironically finding shelter back under the oak-tree with old Jane.

So here, too, the ghosts walk at midnight; but here they walk back into life, there is nowhere to pursue them beyond the tomb. Jack's ghost is nothing without its animal life, and his wandering becomes a constancy of its own; but *not* a fixity or a stability. This is not a reconciliation, but a paradox, a finding of permanence in the most transient of experiences, which is expanded in the fourth song, 'Crazy Jane and Jack the Journeyman'. The door that is left unlatched to let love in, simply lets it out again, and Jack will always go as well as come. So love is '*but* a skein unwound/Between the dark and dawn'. The alternative is the permanence of God, the leap after death into the light which was lost on the soul's first entry into mother's womb. But that sound neo-Platonic doctrine, directly suggesting 'Byzantium', is frustrated before it begins by the stress on its loneliness, and dissipated in the ambiguity of the last two lines:

> Shall leap into the light lost
> In my mother's womb.

It is not possible to determine whether Jane's leap will be towards the light, or more characteristically away from it back into the womb for a constant flux of re-birth (which is equally a Platonic idea). Even the possibility of Jane accepting such a loneliness depended entirely on 'love's skein upon the ground,/My body in the tomb'. In the last stanza she shifts her position only slightly, to a more immediate loneliness 'In an empty bed', and the skein becomes known unambiguously as one which will not be discarded: the passionate intensity unwound between the dark and dawn will draw the ghost back when dead.

The skein unwound between dark and dawn is also a skein unwound between death and life, and therefore a version of Hades' bobbin that may unwind the winding path. But the stress is still as different as the tone, for here we regard man far more than shade, whereas in 'Byzantium' it is stated, and felt, to be 'Shade more than man'. It is patent that the image floating in stanza 2 of 'Byzantium' should have a permanence remote indeed from Jack the Journeyman's occasional visits to Jane's 'bed'. The image itself is produced in stanza 3:

> Miracle, bird or golden handiwork,
> More miracle than bird or handiwork.

The opening lines echo very exactly the syntactic formula of the opening of stanza 2; but image, man or shade is transposed into 'Miracle, bird or golden handiwork'. Miracle plies between bird and handiwork as image did between man and shade. The terms have changed because this is the image itself, the golden bird; the miraculous relation is between bird and golden handiwork, between a natural thing and a thing superlatively made—a work of art in the strictest sense, and therefore free of the mutability of birth and death. But equally it is no mere imitation of a bird, because the insistence on 'miracle' finds in the image at once the quality of life *and* the quality of permanence. It is 'bird or handiwork' according to how you regard it; but more miracle than either, because both at once.

That appears like a moment of achievement in the poem. After the grey, ghostly, indefiniteness of the last stanza, this is concrete, definite, and golden. But some indefiniteness clings to the word 'Miracle' and it becomes a matter of urgency to know more. Problems arise at once in

> Planted on the star-lit golden bough

'Planted' can simply mean 'put', which is necessary since it is not bird enough to fly there; but it also means 'planted' as a tree is planted, suggesting an organic growth forever denied to golden handiwork. There is a similar irony in 'star-lit golden bough', because in star-light a golden bough appears no different from an ordinary bough; to echo a pun in the first stanza, the star-light distains the gold.[1] It can be argued that these ambiguities sustain the miracle; but the need for them also suggests limitation, and we are not altogether surprised to find the bird uttering no nightingale's song, but a cock's crow, and a cock of Hades at that. The frustration implied there is intensified in

> Or, by the moon embittered, scorn aloud . . .

The words recall the first stanza, but the tone has changed. 'Scorn' remembers 'disdains', but it is less dignified, and it is aloud in contrast to the great silence that followed the gong. Such shrill tones belong to Crazy Jane, but the difference is that what in her is a delight becomes here menacing and repugnant; and what they scorn are of course opposites. Starlight and moonlight, too, are now distinguished by the heavy stress on 'Or' which connects them, whereas before they seemed to be indifferently related. Although their light is superficially similar, the constancy of the stars is contrasted with the changeability of the moon. So it becomes important that *both* disturb the golden bird: possessing neither, it is provoked by the constancy of star-light and embittered by the changing moon, symbol of sensuality. In that light, cocks of Hades becomes a latent phallic pun, scorning aloud

---

[1] When first printed line 5 read 'distains', and there is MS support for both forms. In speed the words are usually indistinguishable.

In glory of changeless metal
Common bird or petal
And all complexities of mire and blood.

The movement of these lines is strange, because whilst the bird
regains much of its splendour, its aristocratic contempt for 'common' bird or petal rebounds: it is they that become attractive, and
invite the perception that though complexities of mire and blood
may lack the priapic glory of changeless metal, they are not condemned, as it is, to sterility. The nightingale turned cock is on the
way to the hunched heron of Crazy Jane's frustrated Bishop.

In other words, the golden bird is not meaningful without the
living bird, and the miracle, though real, cannot float free of its
components, bird and golden handiwork. Equally, it must be said
that a work of art, though powerful, is also impotent; and that is
peculiarly apparent in the very formalized art of Byzantium; its
mosaics are not immediately 'moving' as the sensuality of the
renaissance is. Impotent, too, is a world of spirits divorced from
bodies.

So in stanza 4, the golden bird does not prove, after all, to be the
single definitive image; it gives way in its turn to the dance. The
movement of blood-begotten spirits into a dance through which
they are transformed into flame is superbly done, and however the
image has been changed, the idea of a work of art is still sustained.
But it is stranger and more difficult than just that. 'Where all
complexities of fury leave' moves through 'Dying into a dance'
into 'An agony of trance' and insists on the agony by repeating it
in the last line. The dance which offers to distill the spirits from the
furies of complexity begins in its turn to take on the condition
of dervishes; and at the same time that the violence emerges (as
with the embittered bird) the impotence is hinted again in 'cannot',
'An agony of flame that cannot singe a sleeve.'

At this point the tension between 'flame', 'agony' and 'dance' is
perfectly achieved and almost establishes its own stasis. Almost but
not quite, because agony is emerging so strongly and is sustained in
the destructive violence of the last stanza. It is a tension between
attraction and repulsion, or rather between pleasure and pain,

stillness and violent movement. In coming to that, the poem has moved through a remarkable but obscure compression to a position seemingly far removed from common human experience. It is, I think, too easy to lose contact with it. That it has still a relationship with living experience may become clearer via the last of the Crazy Jane poems, 'Crazy Jane Grown Old Looks at the Dancers':

> I found that ivory image there
> Dancing with her chosen youth,
> But when he wound her coal-black hair
> As though to strangle her, no scream
> Or bodily movement did I dare,
> Eyes under eyelids did so gleam;
> *Love is like the lion's tooth.*

> When she, and though some said she played
> I said that she had danced heart's truth,
> Drew a knife to strike him dead,
> I could but leave him to his fate;

The murderous game that is 'heart's truth' in love is obviously part of Crazy Jane's world; and it is far more dangerous than any game, the murderous hate in the intensity of love. The tension of agony and stasis in 'Byzantium' is not the same thing, but it is of the same kind, and they are related in the simultaneous chaos and order of a dance.

But I said that the stasis in the fourth stanza was, like the image in the third, not quite perfect. The stress on agony is growing, and leads into the extraordinary violence that opens the last stanza:

> Astraddle on the dolphin's mire and blood,
> Spirit after spirit! The smithies break the flood,
> The golden smithies of the Emperor!
> Marbles of the dancing floor
> Break bitter furies of complexity,

Dolphins—like the sea itself—symbolize sensual life, so the dolphins carry the blood-begotten spirits through the sea to the purely spiritual world of the holy city. The two distinct images of the third and fourth stanzas, the golden bird and the dance of flame, are finally brought together, but in a way which hardly seems to represent their achievement. The latent force of frustration is released in a fury that is no less bitter than the furies of complexity: the violence of smithy and dancing floor that creates the works of art destroys the living creatures that they are made out of. The serene image floating between man and shade has, after all, destroyed the man on which it depends. Crazy Jane, I suggested, in the fourth song leapt gladly back into the flux of birth and re-birth; 'Byzantium' has been a tremendous effort to envisage an escape from it, to create images that are 'Shade more than man, more image than a shade.' But the closer they are brought to concrete definition the less stable they appear, and what is first perceived as a traffic between sensual and spirit life becomes a violent hostility almost destroying both; and what it creates is not the spirit world but 'Those images that yet/Fresh images beget,' and so once more the world of life, 'That dolphin-torn, that gong-tormented sea.'

But what is most striking here is the radical change of tone in those last three lines: from the exclamatory rhetoric of fury and violence the poem recoils to the extreme quietude[1] of

> Those images that yet
> Fresh images beget,
> That dolphin-torn, that gong-tormented sea.

The emergence carries a sense of relief, and this is encouraged by 'Fresh images'. But the encouragement is not facile: in one sense, 'fresh' only means 'more', and at one stage of its composition Yeats wrote 'more'; in an even earlier draft the line reads '*Worse* images beget',[2] and that sense still remains in the final version, carrying an exhausted despair that the endless cycle has not been broken, that the sea remains torn and tormented. But 'fresh' in its positive sense allows a creative hint, a quality of living forms that

[1] Fraser registers this as 'the triumphantly mounting rhythm' which is certainly possible, though I do not hear it so; we do not differ substantially in understanding of the lines, and perhaps the rhythm is as ambiguous as the meaning.

[2] See Curtis Bradford, 'Yeats's Byzantium Poems: A Study of their Development', *PMLA* (1960).

the most perfect work of art (or spirit) cannot achieve. This tenuous balance between despair and creative relief is sustained, it seems to me, in the last line where the stress naturally falls on 'dolphin' and 'gong', so that 'torn' and 'tormented', though recognized, remain finally unstressed. After the increasingly feverish vision of the last three stanzas, we can understand how Yeats, 'ill again, warmed myself back into life with "Byzantium".'

A balance as delicate and subtle as that is necessarily obscure; there is no such obscurity about applying Yeats' comment on Crazy Jane, 'in memory of those exultant weeks', to what is perhaps the most exultant, as it is also the most characteristic, of the songs, 'Crazy Jane Talks with the Bishop':

> I met the Bishop on the road
> And much said he and I.
> 'Those breasts are flat and fallen now,
> Those veins must soon be dry;
> Live in a heavenly mansion,
> Not in some foul sty.'
>
> 'Fair and foul are near of kin,
> And fair needs foul,' I cried.
> 'My friends are gone, but that's a truth
> Nor grave nor bed denied,
> Learned in bodily lowliness
> And in the heart's pride.
>
> 'A woman can be proud and stiff
> When on love intent;
> But Love has pitched his mansion in
> The place of excrement;
> For nothing can be sole or whole
> That has not been rent.'

Like 'Byzantium', the second stanza makes an abstract, conceptual statement of what stanza 3 presents in decidedly physical terms:

> 'Fair and foul are near of kin,
> And fair needs foul,' I cried.

becomes

> But Love has pitched his mansion in
> The place of excrement;

In exploring this stress the whole song is a development from the refrain of song V, *'All things remain in God'*, and what, here, Jane means by 'Learned in bodily lowliness/And in the heart's pride' is more fully stated in the last stanza of that song:

> I had wild Jack for a lover;
> Though like a road
> That men pass over
> My body makes no moan
> But sings on:
> *All things remain in God.*

The last stanza of 'Crazy Jane Talks with the Bishop' is, Donne-like, close-packed with puns. The interplay of 'sole and whole' with 'soul' and 'hole' is obvious, but the process is continuous from the beginning: 'proud' and 'stiff' mean roughly the same thing applied to grand ladies, but 'proud' is also used of a bitch on heat, and 'stiff' is a common word for tumescence. These puns enforce the tone of this poem in a way that is not obscure. They prelude, however, another line of verbal play with a rather different dimension, one which derives from the dialogue with the Bishop. 'Love', thus capitalized, is the god of love; and simultaneously the pagan god and the Christian one. 'Mansion' is a biblical word, so is 'pitched' (and so, incidentally, is 'whole'). But, normally, you pitch a tent, not a mansion, and before Solomon built the Temple, the Lord, as he explained to David, dwelt in tent or tabernacle. The place of excrement is Cupid's heavenly mansion, and that is one answer to the Bishop; another is that Christ was born in a stable. It follows that 'rent' in the last line is not only the tearing of the hymen when a virgin becomes (w)hole, but also the rending of the veil in the Temple at the moment of Christ's death. In this way the stanza doubles all its references to both gods of Love, trafficking between the two as both opposite and identical, and answering the Bishop either way. Christ's miracles made men and women 'whole', so that Christ and Crazy Jane lie close together here. But the Bishop is excluded, like the priest in Blake, as alien to both. I cannot accept Denis Donoghue's objection that the Bishop is an Aunt Sally, except in the sense that in folk song the antagonist is always an Aunt Sally or nearly so, as the language always lies close to cliché. Jane evidently has affinities with Mary Magdalene, of whom Christ said 'Her sins, which are many, are forgiven; for she loved much . . .'; but Jane's pride will forever defy forgiveness; it is not a question of failing to achieve reconciliation, but of repudiating it.

St Luke's words on Christ's death are: 'And the sun was darkened, and the veil of the Temple was rent in the midst', and St Matthew adds that 'graves were opened; and many bodies of the saints which slept arose . . . and went into the Holy City'. The holy city there is, of course, Jerusalem not Byzantium. Jerusalem was the city where Christianity sprang out of Judaism; Byzantium (not Rome) where it was re-united with Greek paganism. It is not perhaps obvious that 'Byzantium' deals in Christian images, although it was the great Cathedral gong which summoned us through midnight, the cathedral of S. Sophia, the Greek wisdom in the Christian temple. In Crazy Jane it is Platonism that is more obscure, though it is explicit in the second song, 'Crazy Jane Reproved'; her relationship with holiness is primarily via the biblical images of her Irish upbringing by the Irish Bishop.

The relationship I have tried to show between 'Byzantium' and Crazy Jane is that in both these there is a trafficking between body and soul. This is not always obvious about Crazy Jane, so I have laboured to point it out. It is, on the other hand, quite obvious about 'Byzantium', except that it seems to deal far more with spirits than with bodies; it is, in fact, part of its terrifying force that it does so. It is an immensely impressive poem that is also terrifying and repugnant. Crazy Jane's sexuality may have disturbed our prudish streak in the 1950's, but it is indeed heart's truth (and we all know it). So is 'Byzantium'. It will never be built on Ireland's mountains green; nor will Jane ever take a package tour to the Bosphorus. They are worlds apart; yet they are both worlds that every body and soul inhabits; and they should be celebrated.

Against the polite versing of recent English poetry they may appear as rhetorical extravagances; but the truth is that they are statements, not exaggerations, of experience; 'figured foorth', as Sidney put it, in their opposite forms: when all the explanation and evasion is done, 'Byzantium' *is* a tragic ode,[1] and Crazy Jane *is* a bawdy ballad. Each is complete, perfect in itself—and sheer opposite to the other. A single imagination must encompass both, but 'whoever tries to reconcile them', as Blake said, 'seeks to destroy existence'. The world *must* be torn to pieces by the energy of the great creators.

[1] The twin ode, 'Sailing to Byzantium', is not tragic: in its serene conclusion it hints at a comic triviality which returns us to the delighted sensuality of the young in its first stanza, just as the end of 'Byzantium' returns us with fresh attention to the torn and tormented sensuality of drunks and tarts.

VI

The Poem in Transmitted Text—
Editor and Critic[1]

J. E. CROSS

SOME twenty years ago Dr Kenneth Sisam reminded us[2] cogently that all the major Old English poems are extant only in texts at varying removes of transmission. By analysing samples from those few poems which are copied in two manuscripts he demonstrated certain variations between the two texts and therefore errors in one of the two, and sometimes in both. Obviously such kinds of errors as were clearly revealed in these texts could be presumed to exist in the single texts of the remaining poems in the four main poetic codices. Dr Sisam, of course, intended to refute the opinion that a manuscript reading should be defended at all costs, or even at extreme cost. One of his illustrative emendations has been debated and a manuscript reading defended by E. G. Stanley (*R.E.S.*, 1954, pp. 55–8), yet such discussion is surely what he would have wished, since, as he said (p. 42) 'a proper respect for the manuscripts is consistent with a critical and independent attitude towards their evidence. Nothing is to be gained by judging them with a hostile bias'. Nevertheless, 'when, as is usual for Old English poetry, only one late witness is available, there is no safety in following its testimony'. 'The judge [the editor] must not surrender it [his judgement] to the witness' (p. 39).

While agreeing with this conclusion, which demands that both

[1] This paper was read at the International Conference of Professors of English at Dublin, 1968, in the section on Textual Criticism. For some, as yet undivulged, reason, the Irish editors changed their intention of publishing the proceedings. I now have felt free to allow Kenneth Muir to read the paper and I am happy to publish under his general editorship.

[2] *R.E.S.*, XXII (1946), p. 257 seq. reprinted in K. Sisam, *Studies in the History of Old English Literature*, (Oxford, 1953), pp. 29–44. Page references in the text are to the reprint.

defence of a manuscript reading and emendation be judicial although permissible, we may yet wish to change the metaphor since the kind of cross-examination to be given to the manuscript may be more appropriate to an accused prisoner who, under British Law at least, is innocent until proven guilty. This is especially noteworthy when considering poems in single transmitted texts. No editor, I suspect, would have proposed to emend the celebrated verse of Cædmon's *Song of Creation* from *ylda bearnum* ('for children of men') to *eorðan bearnum* ('for children of earth'), if there had not been a second group of manuscripts offering 'the more difficult reading'.[1] In general statement—however acute, careful, experienced and yet bold the editor, it is unlikely that he can recover the poet's words at every half-line from single transmitted texts, and some guilty phrases will remain because they appear to be innocent. As a result, the poem of *Beowulf*, to us, can be no more than that single copy in the manuscript, edited to the best of our human ability.

Dr Sisam asked for a responsible and alert attitude from the editors of Old English texts, but he was also making an important point for critics of the poems which are textually fragile at some points. There is, admittedly, some difference of ultimate function, but both editors and critics are concerned with the sense of the poem. Every poem has its own sense, not necessarily common sense or, for a medieval poem, our modern kind of sense, but nevertheless, a sense which it is part of an editor's and critic's task to discern. The editor, obviously, has to make a decision on every detail of that sense. The critic, who is often more concerned with broader patternings, need not do this, although he should be aware of, and consider, all points of detail. It is scarcely important to a critic, for example, whether Beowulf stood on the hearth or in the interior when he greeted Hroðgar;[2] nor, to take one of Dr

---

[1] See C. L. Wrenn's textual analysis in 'The poetry of Cædmon', *Proceedings of the British Academy*, XXXIII (1946).

[2] *Beowulf* 404. The manuscript reads *heoðe* (interior?), but the common emendation is *heorðe* (hearth). This innocuous example is chosen because a word may have to be considered by a critic on other grounds than of meaning alone, but the difference in the reading of this word can scarcely affect the aesthetic evaluation of *Beowulf*.

Sisam's own examples (p. 40), does it matter for the meaning at least, that the verb *sēcan* (*Genesis A* 1448) is left dangling without an object against the norm of Old English idiomatic practice since the statement in which this occurs repeats an idea which is presented immediately before. Indeed, the OE. poetic figure of variation often helps a critic in his search for poetic sense when the text at some minor points is uncertain.

But the good critic of Old English poetry has always to concern himself with good editorial opinion and practice, and has to equip himself to test that opinion, just as he incessantly tests the opinions of lexicographers against the examples of the words used when placed back in their original contexts and may offer suggestions to them. When, some years ago, a critic (B. Huppé, *Doctrine and Poetry*) flouted the probabilities of good editorial deduction on Cædmon's *Song of Creation* and built an explanatory structure on what was manifestly a bad text, his criticism was vitiated partly because, for this poem, he was not a good editor.

In the course of his essay Sisam showed what a good editor should be, by his own illustrations and by direct statement. His best gift, he said in another paper, is 'a feeling for Anglo–Saxon expression' (p. 45), by which, I take it, he means, a feeling for Old English idiom or linguistic practice, or alternatively, a feeling for *how* the Anglo–Saxons present ideas. Dr Sisam was, of course, speaking to editors and choosing his illustrations for this, but, I missed any real emphasis on one other major editorial quality—a feeling for *what* the Anglo–Saxons are saying. As a good critic should also be a good editor, so the converse obtains. Like the critic the editor should concern himself with what the poet is doing in the whole poem; he should comprehend the poet's range of cultural ideas from the hints and emphases of the poem; he should realize what the poet is selecting and using from this, and he should bear this in mind even when deciding on points of detail.

My first and major illustration is a consideration of the opening passage of *The Old English Phoenix*, where the poet is describing the Earthly Paradise, home of the bird. Within the first thirteen lines there have been two points of editorial debate, emendations proposed and manuscript reading defended, and some explanatory discussion. The passage is presented with a literal translation before indicating the points of debate, although, obviously, a critical and editorial choice is made in text and translation.

> Hæbbe ic gefrugnen   þætte is feor heonan
> eastdælum on   æþelast londa,
> firum gefræge.   Nis se foldan sceat
> ofer middangeard   mongum gefere
> folcagendra,   ac he afyrred is
> þurh meotudes meaht   manfremmendum.
> Wlitig is se wong eall,   wynnum geblissad,
> mid þam fægrestum   foldan stencum.
> Ænlic is þæt iglond,   æþele se wyrhta,
> modig, meahtum spedig,   se þa moldan gesette.
> Đær bið oft open   eadgum togeanes,
> ohnliden hleoþra wyn,   heofonrices duru.

[I have heard that, far from here, in eastern parts, there is the noblest of lands, well-known to men. That region of the earth is not accessible to many men throughout the world, but it is removed from malefactors through the power of the Creator. The whole plain is beautiful, blessed with delights, with the fairest fragrances of the earth. The island is unique, noble the Maker, high-minded, abounding in power, who established the land. The door of heaven is often open towards the blessed there, the best of melodies revealed.]

The first suggested emendation was for *folcāgendra*,[1] but this suggestion may be discounted on normal editorial grounds, since *folcāgende* is extant elsewhere referring to people who are also called *boldāgende* (literally 'a house-owner') and *hæleð* ('a hero, a man'), and it would seem that our word could be another poetic alternative for 'man'.[2] One explicator, O. F. Emerson,[3] has how-

---

[1] viz *foldagendra*; as noted in *The Exeter Book* ed. G. P. Krapp and E. V. K. Dobbie, *The Anglo-Saxon Poetic Records*, III (New York, 1936), p. 272. Poetic texts quoted below are from this edition.

[2] The words all occur in a passage in *Beowulf* 3111–3114 where Wiglaf is asking 'heroes, leaders, men' to fetch wood for Beowulf's funeral pyre not, one might think, a task for leaders alone.

[3] *R.E.S.*, II (1926), p. 22.

ever considered the compound in terms of its elements, literally 'holders, owners of people', that is 'rulers', and proposes this meaning here, since the poet is echoing the Scriptural conception of Paradise as the 'home of the lowly'. An editor, A. S. Cook,[1] takes the whole phrase 'nis—mongum gefere/folcagendra' as an instance of the common Old English poetic figure of litotes or understatement, and would thus translate 'is not accessible to any men'.

The second suggested emendation was for *hlēoþra*, being *hlēodora* (noted in Krapp–Dobbie, p. 272), an unrecorded but permissible compound meaning 'protecting doors', so that the whole phrase would be a tautological variant of the preceding one, i.e. 'The door of heaven is often open, the best of protecting doors unclosed, towards the blessed there'. The emendation was made because the editor did not accept the sense of the manuscript sentence, and this seems to have disturbed all the other editors except Mr Blake, although they all retain the manuscript reading.

A third point is one of editorial explanation where A. S. Cook thought that *īglond* should not mean 'island' in this context but 'land overseas', 'land reached by crossing water'.

But let us consider the poet's general attitude and all his acts. As we have known for a long time the Old English poet is drawing for information on Lactantius's poem *De Ave Phoenice*, at times echoing its statements, sometimes adapting its comments, omitting some Latin detail and yet extending the Latin poem vastly, although using it as a framework for his own order of ideas. The thirteen Old English lines have contact only with the first two Latin lines:[2]

> Est locus in primo felix oriente remotus
> Qua patet aeterni maxima porta poli

[1] A. S. Cook, *The Old English Elene, Phoenix and Physiologus* (New Haven, London, 1919), p. 102; also N. F. Blake, *The Phoenix* (Manchester, 1964), p. 64.
[2] Quoted from Lactantius, *Opera Omnia*, ed. S. Brandt and G. Laubmann, *Corpus Scriptorum Ecclesiasticorum Latinorum*, XXVII, I (Leipzig, 1897), II, I.

[There is a blessed land, afar off in the extreme East, where the great door of the eternal heaven stands open.]

and, anticipatingly, with the Latin line 5 where the land is called 'a plain' (*planities*), although this concept is presented more fully later in the Old English poem (in the same order of ideas as the Latin).

Both Lactantius and the Old English poet are describing the Earthly Paradise, a real place to medieval people and later marked on maps, and a place which is not to be confused here with the Paradise which is our Heaven. By his extensions on the Latin the Anglo–Saxon reveals his extra knowledge of the Earthly Paradise, and shows that he knows what Lactantius is describing. The land is full of fragrance, a cliché in descriptions of the place, but not in Lactantius. It is also an island. As H. R. Patch says:[1] 'it (the Earthly Paradise) is cut off from man because it is located on a high mountain, or by the ocean, or by a fiery wall, or by more than one of these, making it an island'. So, at this point, we may disregard A. S. Cook's editorial explanation of *īglond* (although etymologically possible and still permissible in context) and accept the common meaning of the word as 'island'.

The Englishman, however, also changed the Latin poetic phraseology and adapted ideas to suit his general purpose which was, as I have argued elsewhere,[2] to demonstrate the symbol of the Phoenix within Christian faith to an Anglo–Saxon audience by means of the medieval fourfold method of interpretation. The passage under analysis is within the historical or literal interpretation, and some adaptations are made to place the bird and its home within Christian reality. The English poet certainly transferred the story from the Classical mythological to the Christian conception of world-history. Lactantius had said (11–14) that the Earthly Paradise was not harmed by the fires of Phaeton or the waters of Deucalion. The Englishman accepts the past Flood without naming it:

[1] H. R. Patch, *The Other World* (Camb. Mass., 1950), p. 153, and see Chapter v for the fragrance.

[2] 'The Conception of *The Old English Phoenix*' in *Old English Poetry: Fifteen Essays*, ed. R. P. Creed (Providence, Rhode Island, 1967), pp. 129–152.

Swa iu wætres þrym
ealne middangeard   mereflod þeahte,
eorþan ymbhwyrft,   þa se æþela wong,
æghwæs onsund,   wið yðfare
gehealden stod   hreora wæga,
eadig, unwemme,   þurh est godes   (41–46);

[when, formerly, the surge of water, the sea-flood, covered the whole world, the expanse of the earth, then the noble plain remained protected, entirely unharmed against the rush of the fierce waves; blessed, unmarked, through the grace of God],

but, as a Christian, he can recognize no historical world-fire, and he changes the Latin past tense to a present-future:

bideð swa geblowen   oð bæles cyme,
dryhtnes domes,   þonne deaðreced,
hæleþa heolstorcofan,   onhliden weorþað

(47–49),

[it shall remain flourishing thus until the coming of the fire, the judgement of the Lord, when the halls of death, the tombs of men, shall be opened].

The direct identification and the echo of Apocalypse xx, 13 make it obvious that this is the future fire of judgement, as it is in another phrase:

ne him lig sceþeð
æfre to ealdre,   ærþon edwenden
worulde geweorðe..   (39–41),

[nor shall flame injure them (the trees of the Earthly Paradise) for ever, before a change befall the world].

That change will come with the final doom:

þæt onwended ne bið
æfre to ealdre,   ærþon endige
frod fyrnegeweorc   se hit on frymþe gescop   (82–84),

[that will not be changed for ever before He, who created it in the beginning, end the ancient work of former days].

Relevantly these statements reiterate that the paradise is earthly not heavenly since Christian Anglo–Saxons, unlike some men of the Renaissance, could not believe that the heavens would be destroyed.[1] When the signs of doom appeared in the heavens they knew there were 'þa getimbru þe no tydriað' [*Guthlac A* 18] (structures which never decay) in their heavenly home.

It is now time to recall Emerson's suggestion that some men barred from this land were 'rulers', and reject it as irrelevant in its supporting reason. The scriptural analogy which he cites refers to the difficulty of the powerful and rich in reaching the Heavenly Paradise and our poet is consistently clear that his comments are about the Earthly Paradise.

The Anglo–Saxon, following Lactantius a little later, also positions his land within the cosmos. It is twelve fathoms (or cubits) above the highest earthly mountain, so high, in fact that it was not harmed by the Flood, and thus it is the nearest place on earth to heaven. And, in extension of Lactantius, he places the paradise within the eschatological belief of some Christians when he says:

> The door of heaven is often open towards the blessed
> there, the best of melodies revealed.

The concept of 'the door of heaven' is obviously taken from Lactantius, but it is not merely a poetic figure. Isidore,[2] for example, could refer to real 'doors of heaven' (where the sun goes in and out). Also, 'melody in heaven' is both a scriptural and Old English poetic commonplace which could be accepted realistically by medieval men. If the poet is also talking medieval sense about the blessed in the Earthly Paradise, editorial perplexity and critical confusion may be dispelled.

As may be suspected, it appears that he is. Where the good go

---

[1] See J. E. Cross, 'Aspects of Microcosm and Macrocosm in Old English Literature', *Studies in Old English Literature in honor of Arthur G. Brodeur*, ed. S. B. Greenfield (Oregon, 1963), pp. 1–22.

[2] *Etymologiarum Libri*, xx, lib. XIII cap. i §7.

after death and before judgement day was a debated problem in early Christian times especially in terms of the dogma of Christ's Harrowing of Hell, and some felt that Abraham's Bosom should be removed from Hades. There was ambiguity in the naming of paradise, whether heavenly or earthly, to which the good might go, and some divergence and confusion about the location of paradise. But certain named authorities and some popular texts appeared precise enough for the popular tradition to make unambiguous statements. Origen said (*De principiis* II, xi, 6–7): 'I think that the saints ... when they depart from this life, will remain in some place situated on this earth which the Divine Scriptures call Paradise.' Tertullian thought (*De Resurrectione Carnis*, cap. XLIII) that the martyrs were immediately lodged in paradise, defined (*Apologia*, cap. XLVII) as a place 'appointed to receive the spirits of the saints, separated by a wall or a fiery zone from the knowledge of the world', and identified elsewhere (*De Patientia*, cap. v) as the paradise from which Adam was rejected. Apocryphal legends also make their point. In *The Apocalypse of Paul*, the souls of the righteous go to the earthly paradise after death, situated by Oceanus, the river-sea which surrounds the earth. In this text the earthly is distinguished from the heavenly paradise which is in the third heaven.

Certainly such a belief seeped into the Old English popular tradition, uncomplicated by theological argument. The Old English prose text of the Phoenix (which has no immediate connection with our poem) states baldly:

þær wuneð on godes ængles unrim mid þan halgen
sawlen oðð domes dæig,

[therein dwell a host of God's angels with the holy souls until doomsday].

A similar idea is probably indicated in the prose *Adrian and Ritheus*, that curious mixture of scriptural, apocryphal, gnomic and pseudo-scientific lore, where the answer to the question:

Saga me hwær scyne seo sunne on niht?

is

Ic þe secge on þrim stowum, ærest on þæs hwæles
innoðe þe is cweden leuiathan *and* on oðre tid heo
scynð on helle [and] þe ðridda tid heo scynð on
þam ealond þæt is gl-ð (so MS.) nemned *and* þar
restað haligra manna sawla oð domesdæig.

[Tell me where the suns shines at night? I tell you in three places:
first on the belly of the whale which is called Leviathan, and for
the second period it shines on hell, and for the third period it
shines on the island which is called Gl-ð and there the souls of
holy men rest until doomsday].

It thus appears that a critical approach, which arranges the detail
against the broader picture, although creating that broader picture
with the detail, may allow us to say that the statements in the
manuscript are consistent, medievally sensible and clear. We may
now discount the second emendation and also A. S. Cook's
suggestion that 'nis . . . mongum gefere folcagendra' is the figure
of litotes since some men do attain the Earthly Paradise, at least
their souls do.

My last and minor illustration is from *The Exile's Prayer* or
Resignation in *The Exeter Book*, a poem which offers a problem of
detail to a critic, where no editor has indicated any misgiving, but
perhaps he should have done. Critics' sins are often those of com-
mission, but editors may commit sins of omission in glossing over
phrases which may appear doubtful in context. We need not ask
them to emend, but at least to say 'I do not understand' so that a
later reader's attention is called to the point.

Since E. G. Stanley's illuminating critical analysis of the poem
(*Anglia*, LXXIII, 1955), where, in passing, he solved some textual
problems by explaining the meaning and connotation of some
debated phrases, we should agree that the poem is related to
penitential literature. The speaker is a Christian who first prays
for God's grace and aid. He is sinful but he has striven for God's
favour. It appears that he is ready for death; he seeks 'a life after the
other', 'these transitory days' (31–32). He is 'hastening' to the

'Father of Mankind', 'from this world' (41–42). He offers his prayer for his soul (the *commendatio animae* before death), begging that the devil should not seize it on 'the hated journey' (53), the journey from the body. Like all good Christians, he is afraid for his soul but God's grace gives him courage to hope, and to prepare himself for his *ferðweg* (72), 'the way of the soul', as Professor Stanley rightly identifies the word.

But then he recounts the desolation of his past life, whether figurative or realistic, and it is a doleful tale:

> swa me on frymð gelomp
> yrmðu ofer eorþan,   þæt ic a þolade
> geara gehwylce   (gode ealles þonc!)
> modearfoþa   ma þonne on oþrum,
> fyrhto in folce;   forþan ic afysed eom
> earm of minum eþle.   Ne mæg þæs anhoga,
> leodwynna leas,   leng drohtian
> wineleas wræcca,   (is him wrað meotud)   (84–91),

[since misery came upon me on earth in the beginning so that I ever suffered, year after year, affliction of the mind (thanks be all to God!), fear among men more than anything else; so I have been driven wretched from my home. Thus a man alone, a friendless exile, deprived of the joys of company, can no longer live his life, (the Lord is angry with him)].

From this desolation of exile the speaker suddenly, but not surprisingly, thinks of home:

> ond ymb siþ spræce
> longunge fus   and on lagu þence   (97–98),

[and, eager with longing, I speak about a journey and think of the ocean].

At this point the scribe has overlooked some words, as indicated both by the alliteration and the sense, including a necessary noun which some editors supply:

nat min [sefa]
hwy ic gebycge   bat on sæwe
fleot on faroðe;   nah ic fela goldes
ne huru þæs freondes   þe me gefylste
to þam siðfate,   nu ic me sylf ne mæg
fore minum wonæhtum   willan adreogan   (99–104),

[my [mind] does not know with what I may buy a boat on the
sea, a ship on the wave; I have no gold and indeed no friend who
may help me to the voyage, I myself cannot now fulfill my
desire because of my poverty].

The emphasis in the whole passage is on the wretchedness caused
by the absence of friends from home—so important a motif in
Old English poetry—and by the abject poverty of the man. But
one statement does not seem to fit, although when I mention it, it
will sound like bathos after the high sobriety of the poem. Why, if
the man is so poverty-stricken does he need to *buy* a boat? He only
wants to get home across the sea.

The manuscript text is clear, the whole line alliterates, the half-
lines scan according to normal metrical rules. The editors make no
comment probably because the phrase is sensible in its immediate
small context, but the critic, I think, has the need to ask the question
and to allow the discrepancy to niggle in his mind.

According to the examples and decisions in the standard diction-
aries the translation is accurate. Admittedly, *bycgan* is used for the
hiring of workmen in the vineyard, but 'hiring a boat, a ship' big
enough to cross the sea only lessens the incongruity. The verb may
also be translated 'to get, to procure', but the idea of exchange for
the object is inherent in this use of the word. 'To get a boat'
(by offering money) still leaves us with the difficulty, although
'to get a boat' in Modern English could gloss over it, since
the NE. phrase could mean 'to get a passage on a boat', as 'to get
a train' can mean 'to buy a ticket in order to travel by train'.
But scholarly critics do not gloss over difficulties with ambiguous
translations.

The incongruity remains to the detriment of the poet who
appears to have accepted the phrase merely for alliteration; but

fortunately some evidence exists which clears both scribe and poet from blame.

The, as yet unprinted, Vercelli Homily XIX, a homily for Rogationtide in the two other—also unpublished—texts in which it is copied, includes the story of Jonah and the Ninevites. This account was traditionally associated with the festival since it was a Scriptural parallel to the events at Vienne in Gaul which caused Bishop Mamertus to institute the three-day fast at Rogationtide. The story of Jonah was thus narrated on a number of occasions in early homiletic literature as an example of penitence after a visitation by God, but in no example within my reading more fully than in Vercelli Homily XIX.

In Scripture, in the Douai version, Jonas I, 3 reads:

> And Jonas rose up to flee into Tharsis from the face
> of the Lord: and he went down to Joppe and found a
> ship going to Tharsis. And he paid the fare thereof
> and went down into it, to go with them to Tharsis from
> the face of the Lord.

The Old English homily (in transcript of *The Vercelli Book*) retells this, simplifying by omitting the names of the places:

> ða wolde forþi godes bebodu forfleon ac him com to
> cyððe þæt hie forfleon ne meahte. He þeah on fleame
> wæs oð he to sæ becwom *ond* him þær scip gebohte ond mid
> þam scipmannum him þohte ofer sæ to seglgenne
> (fol. 108v),

[Then he wanted to flee from the commandments of God because of this (his fear of the Ninevites), but it became clear to him that he could not flee from them. Nevertheless, he fled until he came to the sea, and there 'he bought a ship' for himself, and thought to sail across the sea with the sailors].

It appears that 'him þær scip gebohte' is equivalent to the Latin 'dedit naulum ejus' (Vulgate), so that the lexicographers may now record a new idiom, the editors, who were unconscious, may never be worried, and critics may realize that the extreme poverty of the speaker in the Old English poem is appropriately presented since he could not get a boat because he could not 'pay his fare'.

These illustrations, I hope, have re-emphasized that the editor–critic and the critic–editor are one in editing and explicating, especially of poems in single transmitted texts.

VII

The Essential Conrad

NORMAN SHERRY

IN HIS Familiar Preface to *A Personal Record*, that attempt at auto-biography of 1912, Conrad admits to being 'unduly discursive', and certainly few autobiographies have been so apparently dis-ordered and bewildering; seldom has reminiscence followed such a random course of haphazard association. From Poland to Pimlico Square, from the Alps to the Congo, we are led without concern for chronology or geography. And this, we must remind ourselves, is the autobiography of a man whose life did not lack adventure, variety and strangeness. Born in Poland, taken into exile with his parents when he was four, orphaned at the age of eleven, at seventeen alone in Marseilles, sailing to the West Indies, gun-running, gambling, savouring cafe society, in debt, ultimately attempting suicide, at twenty a seaman in the British merchant navy but speaking little English, sailing to India, Australia and the Far East, master of his own ship for two years, steamer captain on the river Congo (from which experience he emerged seriously ill), and finally English author leading the life of an English gentleman in the southern counties, not making a lot from his writing but generally acclaimed, associating with the literary figures of the time—Wells, Galsworthy, Edward Garnett, Ford Madox Ford, tempted to challenge Shaw to a duel, suffering from malarial gout and asthma—in such a life there was ample material for a best-selling autobiography. Yet Conrad dismissed these events in favour of an apparent discursiveness.

[These pages] . . . have been charged with discursiveness, with disregard of chronological order (which is in itself a crime) with unconventionality of form (which is an impropriety). I was told

severely that the public would view with displeasure the infor-
mal character of my recollections. 'Alas!' I protested, mildly.
'Could I begin with the sacramental words, "I was born on such
a date in such a place"? The remoteness of the locality would
have robbed the statement of all interest. (A Familiar Preface,
pp. xx–xxi)[1]

Conrad's deliberate rejection here, and in his novels, of the
accepted chronological order and conventional form is the
characteristic which limited his reading public then and now, but it
is a deliberate rejection with a deliberate purpose. He had earlier
insisted to William Blackwood, his publisher, when the latter
refused to advance him money since the firm made little out of
his work:

I know exactly what I am doing . . . Out of the material of a
boys' story I've made *Youth* by the force of the idea expressed in
accordance with a strict conception of my method . . . I shall not
depart from my method . . . I think it is a true method. All my
endeavours shall be directed to understand it better, to develop
its great possibilities, to acquire greater skill in the handling—to
mastery in short.[2]

And again, taking umbrage at some criticism by Wells, he wrote:
'I will never disguise [my style] in boots of Wells's (or anybody
else's) making . . . I shall make my own boots or perish!'[3] And of
A Personal Record he wrote:

This is but a bit of psychological document . . . these memories
put down without any regard for established conventions have
not been thrown off without system and purpose. They have
their hope and their aim. (A Familiar Preface, pp. xx–xxi)

[1] References throughout are to J. M. Dent and Sons' *Collected Edition of the
Works of Joseph Conrad* (London, 1947).
[2] Letter of 31 May 1902, *Joseph Conrad, Letters to William Blackwood and David
S. Meldrum*, ed. William Blackburn (Duke University Press, 1958), p. 154.
[3] Jocelyn Baines, *Joseph Conrad: A Critical Biography* (London, 1960), p. 167.

His hope was that

> from the reading of these pages there may emerge at last the
> vision of a personality: the man behind the books so funda-
> mentally dissimilar as, for instance, *Almayer's Folly* and *The
> Secret Agent*, and yet a coherent, justifiable personality both in its
> origin and in its action.

The aim was

> to give the record of personal memories by presenting faithfully
> the feelings and sensations connected with the writing of my
> first book and with my first contact with the sea. (p. xxi)

To produce 'a bit of psychological document' that gives the
vision of a personality by presenting faithfully the feelings and
sensations connected with an event is, therefore, Conrad's
'method', the method he defended in his letter to Blackwood. It
varied of necessity from novel to novel, subject to subject, and we
must, I think, take the idea of a 'vision of a personality' in the wider
sense. For Conrad this was only rarely the personality of one man.
Perhaps it was in the case of MacWhirr in *Typhoon*, but usually the
term 'personality' covers much more.

One further point I would like to stress here with regard to this
method and that is Conrad's choice and treatment of the 'significant event'. In the case of his autobiography he wisely selected for a
basis the two significant and pivotal events of his life—going to sea
and writing his first novel. But in recalling these events, his concern
is with the feelings and sensations connected with them—less the
event than the surrounding emotional field, an emotional field that
can be made up of quite varied and disparate elements. The first
three pages of *A Personal Record*, carefully read, give us a revealing
insight into the Conrad who was moving from seaman to novelist.
The number of diverse and varied references bring together the
literary and the sea life in sharp, yet close contrast, and the emotional tone of that period for him derives from the hot cabin, the
secret writing, the memories of Malaya, the inspiration of Flaubert,

the trivial conversation and activities of fellow seamen, and the lack of privacy. Conrad *states* none of this—but he reproduces the emotional field through suggestive and appropriately haphazard detail.

There is nothing in his *definition* of his method that implies analysis of a moral or ethical kind, and in a sense it is this that sets Conrad apart from novelists such as Eliot, Hardy, James and even Lawrence. The examination of motive and conscience within a strong moral and social framework is not his aim. Nor is it his aim to recount simply a significant or interesting story. His avoidance of the obvious climax at times, his convoluted narrative, his confusing time changes are needed to effect his aim, to give 'a bit of psychological document' that presents the vision of a personality. This suggests a method of work which leaves most things open-ended.

His approach to his material stems, I am sure, from Conrad's basic belief about the universe, a belief which he sets out in *A Personal Record*:

> The ethical view of the universe involves us at last in so many cruel and absurd contradictions, where the last vestiges of faith, hope, charity, and even of reason itself, seem ready to perish, that I have come to suspect that the aim of creation cannot be ethical at all. I would fondly believe that its object is purely spectacular . . . The rest is our affair—the laughter, the tears, the tenderness, the indignation, the high tranquillity of a steeled heart, the detached curiosity of a subtle mind—that's our affair! And the unwearied self-forgetful attention to every phase of the living universe reflected in our consciousness may be our appointed task on this earth. (p. 92)

Taking Conrad's work as a whole, we can see that he is attempting this 'unwearied, self-forgetful attention to every phase of the living universe reflected in our consciousness', and since the universe is not ethical, but spectacular, the object of the artist is to reflect as accurately as possible, the spectacular nature of the universe. The writer's task is 'by the power of the written word to make you hear, to make you feel—it is, before all, to make you *see*'. (Author's

Preface to *The Nigger of the 'Narcissus'*, p. x). But he retains 'the detached curiosity of a subtle mind' and his method aims to arouse the same attitude in his reader.

The spectacle, the vision of a personality, is not confined to the central event in Conrad's view, since that would be a false limitation. The spectacle includes the reverberations of that story among all those who were involved, however remotely, even as listeners or as retailers of the event, since they are part of the spectacle, being part of the spectacular universe. It is as though Henry James, instead of taking a tale told to him at a dinner party and then working it up into an enclosed and defined work of art, saw the necessity of revealing to the reader the events of that dinner party, the personalities and reactions involved in the telling of the story, and his own reactions to it. The method has its centre in the essential conception of the truth of the spectacular universe being something that comes to us fragmented, through our senses, affected by our personalities, an accidental, circuitous and undefined truth which is, nevertheless, nearer to the truth as man knows it than the carefully selected and more formally arranged truth of other storytellers.

The narrators are, therefore, part of the spectacle as are the conditions under which the story is told. And just as the evidence, the reactions, are constantly being filtered through other personalities, so we become one of the listeners assessing what is said. And, as listeners, we not only share in the creation since we are present watching the truth being put together, but we also confirm and complete the stories. Conrad's art is a social art—the collaboration of many tellers and many listeners:

> In time the story shaped itself before me out of the listless answers to my questions, out of the indifferent words heard in wayside inns ... people confirmed and completed the story. ('The Idiots', p. 58)

But the aim of the story is the search and not the conclusion. The sensitive reader, responding to the complex emotional field Conrad presents, will not find it a simple task to reach a verdict:

The part of the inexplicable should be allowed for in appraising the conduct of men in a world where no explanation is final. (*A Personal Record*, p. 35)

But the need to adopt a technique which would hold all the elements of his vision in suspension so that the reader would be at once involved and detached brought Leonard Woolf's criticism: 'I had the feeling which one gets on cracking a fine, shining, new walnut . . . only to find that it has nothing inside'.[1] Such a comment indicates that the reader has not made the correct response, has not realized the significance of the shell as well as of the kernel. It is true to say of Conrad what was said of Marlow:

> . . . to him the meaning of an episode was not inside like a kernel but outside, enveloping the tale which brought it out only as a glow brings out a haze, in the likeness of one of these misty halos that sometimes are made visible by the spectral illumination of moonshine (*Heart of Darkness*, p. 48).

Thus in *Lord Jim*, for the personality to be presented fully and accurately, the various viewpoints must be there and held in suspension in all their complexity and their contradictory nature. And to appreciate the complexity of Conrad's vision we must have the straightforward third person account of Jim's life and character up to the *Patna* disaster. After that the field is thrown open so that we can observe, with detachment, the effect of Jim upon all those who come, even remotely, into contact with him. All Marlow's reflections on first seeing Jim point to his immediate emotional involvement with the young mate who had deserted his ship:

> This was my first view of Jim. He looked as unconcerned and unapproachable as only the young can look. There he stood, clean-limbed, clean-faced, firm on his feet, as promising a boy as ever the sun shone on; and, looking at him, knowing all he knew and a little more too, I was as angry as though I had detected him trying to get something out of me by false pretences. He had no business to look so sound. I thought to myself

[1] Review of *Suspense*, *Nation and Athaeum*, 3 October 1925, p. 18.

H

—well, if this sort can go wrong like that . . . and I felt as though I could fling down my hat and dance on it from sheer mortification . . . (p. 40).

Jim offers a threat to the solidity, the truth of Marlow's personal universe. He is 'an up-standing, broad-shouldered youth', firm, promising, 'so typical of that good, stupid kind we like to feel marching right and left of us in life'. Such people about one confirm one's own convictions of the rightness of certain things in the universe. Jim is a threat to all this and so he makes Marlow angry. Beside him are the other rogues from the *Patna*, but Marlow does not 'care a rap' for their behaviour. They are part of his world also, but recognizable, known and therefore easily dealt with. Jim is dangerous because he seems to be 'one of us' and yet is flawed, flawed by a weakness that might easily be considered from another point of view as a strength—he lacks 'a faith invulnerable to the strength of facts, to the contagion of example, to the solicitation of ideas'.

Hang ideas! [says Marlow.] They are tramps, vagabonds, knocking at the back-door of your mind . . . each carrying away some crumb of that belief in a few simple notions you must cling to if you want to live decently and would like to die easy! (p. 43)

Thus Marlow, who appears to be an experienced and knowledgeable observer because of his sea-faring life, is in fact a partial observer since he depends upon a very firmly drawn moral vision of man. His comments later in the novel upon Jim's father, the parson, living in 'that quiet corner of the world as free of danger or strife as a tomb' (p. 342), believing that 'Virtue is one all over the world, and there is only one faith, one conceivable conduct of life, one manner of dying' (p. 341), only reflect back on his own convictions of the 'one conceivable conduct of life'; but Marlow cannot make that comment on himself as an omniscient author might.

Indeed it is possible to look upon Stein as equally fixed in his view of life. The end of his talk about immersing in the 'destructive element' is to treat Jim as one of his specimens and lock him up away from the world in Patusan, away from the destructive element, away from danger: 'Bury him in some sort.' (p. 219) And yet, although Marlow on leaving Patusan feels like a man released from bonds, as if 'a great hand . . . had flung open an immense portal' (p. 331) and he revels in the 'vastness of the opened horizon that seemed to vibrate with a toil of life, with energy of an impeccable world', Jim is not insulated from life in Patusan.

A further criticism of Jim's existence in the Bornean settlement comes from the privileged man:

> You alone, [Marlow writes to him] have showed an interest in him that survived the telling of his story, though I remember well you would not admit he had mastered his fate. You prophesied for him the disaster of weariness and of disgust with acquired honour, with the self-appointed task, with the love sprung from pity and youth. You had said you knew so well 'that kind of thing', its illusory satisfaction, its unavoidable deception. You said also . . . that 'giving your life up to them' [*them* meaning all of mankind with skins brown, yellow, or black in colour] 'was like selling your soul to a brute'. You contended that 'that kind of thing' was only endurable and enduring when based on a firm conviction in the truth of ideas racially our own, in whose name are established the order, the morality of an ethical progress. (pp. 338-9)

Now why was this aspect brought in?

If we attempt to see *Lord Jim* in terms of Conrad's declared method, we are wrong to assume that Jim is the sole aim and object of the story. After all, in spite of Marlow's insistence, is Jim so unclear? Are not his character, personality and fate, in fact, quite clear to the reader? I would suggest that what fundamentally interested Conrad was the effect upon a wide-ranging society of Jim's action, the varied and positive reactions of a number of strong egoisms, and ultimately the ironic conclusion that so much discussion and enquiry elicited only an 'obscure fate', and an impression of humanity ultimately concerned with and trapped in its individual illusions. This is the 'bit of psychological document' of a vision of a personality he had in mind.

Returning to Conrad's letter to Blackwood we find him insisting:

> ... the last pages of *Heart of Darkness* where the interview of the man and the girl locks in—as it were—the whole 3000 words of narrative description into one suggestive view of a whole phase of life, and makes of that story something quite on another plane than an anecdote of a man who went mad in the Centre of Africa.[1]

We must note here that the idea of Marlow's interview with Kurtz's Intended at the end of the story locking in the narrative is a statement of a highly conscious craftsman. But more significant is the suggestion that the narrative produces 'one suggestive view of a whole phase of life'. By this Conrad meant not simply a phase of Marlow's life but a whole phase of man's existence as seen through Marlow's eyes, influenced by his experience of one specific aspect of that phase of existence. The subject is, of course, colonization, which Marlow's preamble traces back to Roman times in Britain and forward to his own experiences on the Congo river. We must see the tale once more as a story of Kurtz viewed as part of Marlow's experience which has become part of the narrator's experience of that evening on the Thames with which the story opens.

The technique throughout the story is to give glimpses, glimpses which constantly move in and out of focus, stretch back and forward in time as though the world is viewed through a telescope which is constantly being regulated. The story begins with the yawl, *Nellie*, floating in the luminous serenity of an evening on the Thames with only the threatening gloom of the city beyond. Those on board look at 'the venerable stream not in the vivid flush of a short day that comes and departs forever, but in the august light of abiding memories' (p. 47). This sense of suspended animation in place and time is symbolic of Conrad's intention in the

[1] *Letters to William Blackwood*, p. 154.

story. The reader also must be placed in this situation, suspended by the various themes of the story so that he can evaluate not only Marlow's account or Kurtz's fate but these stories placed in their historical and universal setting. He is saying, 'Here are all the facts and illusions of this piece of the spectacular universe. You cannot judge Marlow, or Kurtz, or the pilgrims until you have them all before you.'

The narrator gives a glorified vision of the Thames's history, of the men who had sailed from the river bearing 'the torch', 'a spark from the sacred fire'. But Marlow takes up this idea, going farther back in time to the Roman invasion, seeing the river as a Roman soldier must have seen it—

> the very end of the world . . . death skulking in the air, in the water, in the bush . . . the utter savagery . . . all that mysterious life of the wilderness . . . He has to live in the midst of the incomprehensible, which is also detestable. And it has a fascination, too . . . The fascination of the abomination . . . (pp. 49–50).

The telescope re-focuses and we are shown a map of Africa with the river like a snake, and suddenly, with the tale of the murdered captain Fresleven, the focus is on an incident on that river, a story of death and panic. And then we are in the continental city, centre of the great trading enterprise. Marlow sees it as a whited sepulchre, though he admits he might be prejudiced, but he is overcome by the sense of hushed importance that hangs over the trading enterprise, the interest of the doctor in the mental changes the Congo brings about, the enthusiasm of his aunt who sees him as 'an emissary of light', 'a lower sort of apostle'. The vision of a personality in this story, built up by so many glimpses and suggestions, is as complex as that of *Lord Jim*, but it is the personality of an enterprise, an enterprise based on delusion and self-deception. It is doubt and delusion that Marlow brings back with him and to which he finally succumbs when he lies to the Intended to give support to her particular illusion about the man who went mad in Africa. But the essential aspect of the vision, the aspect which forms the framework of the story, objectifying and placing the central action for the reader, is the historical glimpse of human activity with its suggestions of repetition, of the unchanging nature of man, of the fragility of such concepts as 'civilization' and 'progress'. Marlow's experience becomes a closely observed example of a certain type of human activity that is as old as mankind; and Marlow's doubts and bewilderments in this framework become the passing reactions of a contemporary.

The Secret Agent is usually approached as a political novel dealing as it does with an anarchist bomb outrage and the response of 'an embattled society' to it, but I think we should rather approach it from the point of view of Conrad's declared method, when we find that the 'vision of a personality' he is presenting here is not specifically or narrowly a political one. The novel, strangely enough, is prefigured in its essential themes in *Heart of Darkness*, and indeed can be seen as a response to Marlow's comment to his companions on the *Nellie* in that story:

> You can't understand. How could you?—with solid pavement under your feet, surrounded by kind neighbours ready to cheer you or to fall on you, stepping delicately between the butcher and the policeman, in the holy terror of scandal and gallows and lunatic asylums ... (p. 116)

The Secret Agent's aim is to give us a view of the personality of a society outlined here by Marlow. It demonstrates the kind of life lived between the butcher and the policeman and the delicate stepping required in this environment when the balance is threatened by an apparently revolutionary event. The emotional field of the novel revolves about the need for everyone to preserve the balance for fear of the possibility of complete reversal. And the consequences of such a reversal—suggested here—are given in Winnie Verloc's fear of scandal, her terror of the gallows, her final madness. The world of London of the late nineteenth century is as fearful and dangerous in its depths as are the jungles of the Congo. The activity needed to survive is not that of the engineer or the steamboat captain, nor is it necessary to be without entrails— 'Men who come out here should have no entrails' (*Heart of Dark-*

ness, p. 74)—it is the ability to walk delicately. This is Conrad's picture of civilization—the alternative picture to the primitive Congo—where 'going at it blind' would bring disaster.

> The inner truth [says Marlow] is hidden—luckily, luckily. But . . . I felt often its mysterious stillness watching me at my monkey tricks, just as it watches you fellows [the Director of Companies, the Lawyer, the Accountant, etc.] performing on your respective tight-ropes for—what is it? half-a-crown a tumble. (*Ibid.* pp. 93-4)

It is a curious and suggestive fact that the same image appears very significantly in *The Secret Agent* (written six years later) when Inspector Heat, being interviewed by the Assistant Commissioner, is suddenly shaken in his confidence by his superior's probing questions:

> He felt at the moment like a tight-rope artist might feel if suddenly, in the middle of the performance, the manager of the Music Hall were to rush out of the proper managerial seclusion and begin to shake the rope. (p. 116)

The characters in the novel, including the anarchists, are all concerned to continue walking their individual tight-ropes. The Chief Inspector has a dislike 'of being compelled by events to meddle with the desperate ferocity of the Professor' (p. 122); the instinct of self-preservation is strong in the Assistant Commissioner and so he saves Michaelis from prison; for Mr Verloc, the 'whole social order . . . had to be protected against the shallow enviousness of unhygienic labour' (p. 12); the Professor retains his freedom and threat through the explosives he carries; the Lady Patroness is reassured by Michaelis's gentleness; the police and the anarchists preserve a nice balance of interests.

For Conrad this society, then, is a delicately balanced one and its members walk delicately. The waters close over the Verlocs—literally for Winnie, metaphorically for Stevie and Adolf Verloc. Their tragedy is soon forgotten and the anarchists, police and high society continue in their undisturbed way. But the threat remains, the balance can always be turned. To retain this impression of the tight-rope walkers and the depths beneath them, Conrad not only gives us the different attitudes to the Greenwich Outrage of many characters, he also encloses the event in a frame of irony which retains the tension but constantly suggests the possibility of reversal. For Conrad this irony is essential to the presentation of this aspect of the spectacular universe. More strongly than in any other novel, the universe he presents here is ironical. The high ideals of conduct put forward in other novels do not exist here. The characters step delicately to preserve only their own personal safety, their ambitions, their place in society, and ironically, the depths lie just beneath them—not the depths of anarchy and revolution, but the depths of personal tragedy. The first victim is likely to be the sensitive in this world of pain and Stevie, sensitive to the pain of man and of animal, suffers the ultimate in pain, entirely without premonition of his grisly end. Almost twenty years after Conrad's death, Bertrand Russell, in a radio talk, caught with great precision, the essential Conrad notion:

I felt that he thought of civilized and morally tolerable human life as a dangerous walk on a thin crust of barely cooled lava which at any moment might break and let the unwary sink into fiery depths.[1]

But the irony in this novel is also the means by which the whole vision is kept detached and in suspension so that the reader can regard it with detachment and can form his own judgement of the society presented.

There is ironic reversal in terms of the action, reversals which shake the precarious balance of the characters' self-interest. Vladimir's orders to Verloc shatter the Secret Agent's slumbrous existence, and the attempt on the First Meridian accidentally kills Stevie, the only innocent in the novel; the Professor's threat to society only preserves the safety of the Professor; Winnie's attempt to protect her brother through encouraging his devotion to Verloc

[1] 'Portraits from memory, v: Joseph Conrad', *The Listener*, 17 September 1953, p. 462.

and by sewing his address into his overcoat only brings about his death and ensures that the news reaches her in a cold-blooded way; Ossipon's attempt to exploit her as he has exploited other women foreshadows his own madness and despair. The authorial commentary (and there is a great deal in this novel) retains the sense of a delicate balance between appearance and reality, intention and result, morality and expediency, and frequently points to the ironic significances: Mr Verloc is 'steady like a rock—a soft kind of rock', the sun produces a rusty appearance on his overcoat but

Mr Verloc was not in the least conscious [at that moment] of having got rusty (p. 12)

[Mr Verloc] generally arrived in London (like the influenza) from the Continent (p. 6)

[Ossipon] pulled the newspaper out. It was a good-sized, rosy sheet, as if flushed by the warmth of its own convictions, which were optimistic (p. 70)

[the Assistant Commissioner of Police's] suspicion of the police methods (unless the police happened to be a semi-military body organized by himself) was not difficult to arouse ... and his appreciation of Chief Inspector Heat's zeal and ability, moderate in itself, excluded all notion of moral confidence. (p. 115)

Characters are unaware, in spite of their cautious behaviour, of the ironic possibilities underlying their own statements: '"You could do anything with that boy, Adolf," Mrs Verloc said ... "He would go through fire for you"' (p. 184), which is what he does; Winnie's statements are often of this kind for she says to Stevie just before he is blown to pieces, 'You know you do get yourself very untidy when you get the chance' (p. 189); 'The humanitarian hopes of the mild Michaelis', according to the Lady Patroness,

tended not towards utter destruction, but merely towards complete economic ruin of the system. And she did not see where was the moral harm of it. It would do away with the

multitude of the 'parvenus', whom she disliked and mistrusted
... With the annihilation of all capital they would vanish, too;
but universal ruin ... would leave the social values untouched.
The disappearance of the last piece of money could not affect
people of position. She could not conceive how it could affect
her position. (p. 111)

The monstrous town in which Conrad saw this vision is a place
of concealed threats and possible terrifying reversals. It is a town in
which an Assistant Commissioner of Police can transform himself,
with a minimum of disguise, into a foreign anarchist, not only in
appearance, but in spirit.

Because he is showing us a psychological study of a particular
society and its attitudes rather than an analysis of politics, Conrad
deals with the actual explosion only in terms of its effects on these
tight-rope walkers. Again he has not departed from his method.
Out of a thriller plot of anarchy and political intrigue he made *The
Secret Agent* by the force of the idea expressed in accordance with a
strict conception of his method. And his method is firmly and
ironically to present an apparently placid surface where anarchists
talk endlessly, and agents can afford to wallow in bed half the day,
where society ladies entertain ex-prisoners as well as high-ranking
policemen, and where Inspector Heat can exchange the passing
word with the extremist, the Professor; where there are many
signs and tokens, unobserved by the actors, that insanity and madness are in fact part of the prosaic world outside the asylums, an
insanity just below the words spoken or the gestures made.

I have stressed that Conrad's method carries with it little ethical
or moral implication. Admitting the influence, through his method
and technique, of his philosophy of man's position in the universe,
there is no further forcing of the story into a narrower moral
pattern:

The mysteries of a universe made of drops of fire and clods of
mud do not concern us in the least. The fate of a humanity condemned ultimately to perish from cold is not worth troubling
about. If you take it to heart it becomes an unendurable tragedy.
If you believe in improvement you must weep, for the attained

perfection must end in cold, darkness and silence. In a dispassionate view the ardour for reform, improvement for virtue, for knowledge, and even for beauty is only a vain sticking up for appearances as though one were anxious about the cut of one's clothes in a community of blind men.[1]

The conclusions, generally, relate in their implication only to essential action within the novel, to essential individual attitudes, and not to an external morality. The Intended's demand for personal comfort, her certainty that Kurtz thought only of her, carries no moral stigma. Placed as it is, it is simply the expression of her nature and illusion, of her ultimate fear of facing anything beyond her small knowledge of existence. If the tight-rope walker tumbles as a result of the manager shaking the rope, he cannot be blamed morally. He might be praised for agility if he succeeds in keeping his balance, as MacWhirr does, as the narrator in *The Shadow-Line* does. And this is what I mean by referring to the novels as 'open-ended'. There is, because of the method, a sense of men doing what they have to do, and of there being little point in moral judgement afterwards. 'Precious little rest in life for anybody. Better not to think of it,' as Captain Giles says at the end of *The Shadow Line*.

[1] Letter of 14 January 1898, *Joseph Conrad's Letters to R. B. Cunninghame Graham*, ed. C. T. Watts (London, 1969), p. 65.